THE DAY THEY SHOT REVEEN

Stories from a PEI small town

DENNIS KING

Dedicated to a great teller of stories

My father, Lionel MacKenzie King (1929-1996)

'Good stories come from living;

Great stories come from telling.'

The photo on the cover is from the files of Faye Rilley, Georgetown, PEI's unofficial town photographer. The photo shows Charlie Griffin walking on Kent Street in Georgetown in 1966. Charlie was one of the towns' many legendary characters.

Contents

Foreword 3

Introduction 6

Part 1: The Stories of My Dad 14

    A Visit from Nathan Allen? 22

    The Ice Cakes 27

    The Corn Broom 33

Part 2: The Boughton Island Poets' Society 36

    Fair Boughton Isle 37

    Uncle Jack's Wedding Toast 39

    The Georgetown Rink 40

    The Colorful Toast 43

    Helping Her Soldier Come Home 43

    Grandmother's funeral song 43

    The Merchant named Jim 45

    Sage Advice from Uncle Donald 47

Part 3: The King Homestead 51

    The Teapot 53

    The Hateful Bull 57

    Everybody needs a Benji! 64

    Foolishness on the calendar 68

    The Cattie King Royalty Burger 74

    We've got Mark. You guys take Denny 76

    Hungry Hungry Hippos 80

Part 4: There is no place like Georgetown! 84

    The Day They Shot Reveen 85

    Look Dad...It's a Pirate! 91

    Roy and Mae 115

    Dr. Aitken comes to Georgetown 119

Georgetown Santa 123

Jack Daniels and the Dry Heaves 129

Part 5: Georgetown characters 136

Charlie Martell, the Blue Collar Mayor 137

Quite the Bucko was Eloi Doiron 144

The Cowboy Mike Steele 149

Mackey and Sophia 155

The Guy Called Binx MacLean 158

The Long, Ol' Drive with Charlie MacConnell 162

Part 6: Personal favorites and other classics 165

Bobby and the Million 166

A Trip to the Doctor with Stewart MacRae 168

Just Being Forbie Kennedy 172

The Birds and the Bees 176

Exercising Your Watervale Franchise 177

Stretching the Gifted Turkey 179

The Eaton's catalogue 181

Endorsements... 183

Acknowledgements.. 189

Foreword
By Melissa Batchilder

I've known Denny since we were little kids, but in 1970s Georgetown, we were way too cool to talk to each other. I was a few years ahead of him in school and with his childhood aspirations to become a famous road hockey player, our paths didn't often cross - I was having nothing to do with the likes of road hockey.

Rather, I was busy spending after school hours on my father's old saw horses practicing to be a world-class gymnast. The vast distance between our childhood dreams kept us apart until later in life when we were both coming to grips with our dashed hopes of athletic fame by doing what most do when you try to find oneself - you become a reporter for a local newspaper.

It was during that time that I first became familiar with Denny's writing and wondered why I had never talked to that scruffy kid with the snowflake patterned polyester sweaters and droopy jeans. He was so clever! During the course of the next two decades, we danced the path of friendship that only those from small towns do. One step forward, two steps back, trying to figure each other out. Always skeptical of the process, waiting for the hammer to fall or the scam to be revealed. I can safely say it wasn't until a couple of years ago that we finally surrendered and the game was over. We were clearly kindred spirits and it was time to accept we were going to be forever friends.

It was late one night, at my home on the south coast of Massachusetts, when I first read this collection of Denny's stories. With nothing but the moon to brighten up the room, I was sitting in bed, my husband sleeping soundly beside me. I expected to read a few pages and head off to sleep, with plans to finish reading it during the course of the week.

What I didn't expect – although I've bantered through stories with Denny for the better part of four decades – was the vibrating hysterics that would consume me, as I tried hard not to wake my husband. With every line and every reference, I would lose more control of my laughter. I soon realized I would not be able to put the book down until every story was read. I got out of bed and headed downstairs to the kitchen where I wouldn't disturb anyone, and where I could fully ensconce myself in that wondrous feeling of "home" that Denny so brilliantly brings to life in this book.

As you will soon discover, Denny shares on these pages, not just a few things he remembers, he demonstrates the true craft of storytelling. The depth and vivid recall with which he brings every character and scenario to life, is delivered with an immeasurable talent for timing and delivery, that is reserved for the very clever and fortunate few. It's genetics. Nowhere is this more apparent than in the King family.

As a lover of great stories, I've been reading and listening to tales from around the world since I was a child, including the enthralling stories of my own father. I'm one of the many who have had to leave the Island in an effort to make my way in the world. There's not a day that I don't wish it could be different - that I don't wish I could be following Denny's path down the road that runs by the old Brudenell Park and across the ball field behind the jail.

In the meantime, I'll just cling to his stories. My hope is that you will do the same.

Melissa Batchilder is a public relations executive currently residing in Fairhaven, Massachusetts, USA. She was born, and remains forever connected, to Georgetown, PEI, Canada.

Introduction

I have always known there is nothing like a good story.

It is something I learned when I was very young. I used to sit beneath the kitchen table and listen to my father Lionel tell stories to friends and visitors who had come to our home.

Ours was a regular meeting place where many would gather for tea, conversation and entertainment. Inevitably, guests would ask my father to tell some stories. He would never disappoint.

My father's performances were impulsive, never planned. His was an almost reactive oratory that changed with the mood of the room and the coming and going of guests. It would happen with regular innocence. The tea would pour. Conversation would include the news of the day, other local goings-on and eventually would evolve into my father telling a story. My father loved telling stories. And, he was really good at it.

My father's stories were local and organic. They were always about people he knew or had grown up with and they were almost always funny.

Sometimes his stories were short and snappy with a funny punch line. Other times his stories were long and drawn out, and they would branch into sub-plots or anecdotes before coming to a funny conclusion. Without fail, whenever my father told a story, the guests would always roar with laughter and approval. It was pure magic.

Sometimes others would inject a story of their own, as people are prone to do. Their stories would evoke a little chuckle or be met with tepid approval. Not that these were poor tales, mind you, but they seemed to lack the magic of my father's stories.

I used to think this was because others' stories were just not as good as those of my dad. I thought that for a long time, until once I heard my father re-tell a friend's story. He changed the story only slightly, to make it his own, and as they always did, the guests roared with laughter. Same story, but Dad found a way to put the magic into it.

Years later, I asked my dad if he actually lived the stories he told or if he took some poetic license with the details. He just smiled and said, "Son, good stories come from living; great stories come from telling."

His simple secret revealed. Details are important to a good story but the real magic of a great story is in the telling. I have never forgotten that.

For just about as long as I can remember, I have loved listening to and telling stories. I was fortunate to have inherited my dad's keen ear for a story. His brothers Jack and Donald also had it. It is a King family trait. So too are the quick minds, sharp tongues and hearts that blow up before they can become old!

The Kings came from Boughton Island – a tiny island in the mouth of the Cardigan Bay, in eastern Prince Edward Island. As you might imagine, for someone growing up on a remote island off the coast of another Island in the 1920s and 30s, entertainment opportunities were limited.

When they were not doing the family chores, the Kings spent their days trying to outdo one another with stories, poems, jokes, riddles and rhymes. While each had their own unique style, the King clan all shared active imaginations, vivid recall and a cutting wit.

As I think back now to every party or function I ever went to, be it large or small, one of the Kings would end up surrounded by a group of people, and the stories would start and people would laugh. They would laugh hard. People would always leave those little gatherings happy.

I was always impressed with the ability of the King brothers, not just to hold court, but to hold the emotions of the crowd in the palm of their hands. They fed off it. As people laughed, they would stand and smile this broad smile. It was fascinating to watch.

In many ways, I have spent a good part of my life in pursuit of that broad smile. I suppose it is why most entertainers to do what they do. Standing in front of an audience as it erupts into laughter and approval is the most exhilarating feeling I have ever known. The size of the audience is immaterial.

I lost my father in 1996, but I am reminded of him often. When I think of him, I usually find myself smiling as I recall one of the many sayings he had or one of his funny stories. I loved the way my father talked. His twang was endearingly eastern Prince Edward Island. I have also come to appreciate how well thought out and chosen his words were, especially considering the limitations of his Grade 3 education.

For instance, my father would never ask you to help him lift an object. He would say, *"hook on to the end of that with me."* Or, if I asked him for a drink of his beer, he would never just say, "take a sip." He would say, *"take the neck out of that,"* as he passed it to me or, *"take a quick pull of that and give it right back."*

My father would never make a prediction. He would *"prophecise"* the outcome of a game or event. Nobody talks like that anymore. I feel we are somehow worse as a society because of it.

Physically, I am not much like my father. I am built more like my uncles, well-dressed through the middle and arse! My father was slim. He never weighed more than 130 pounds. I weighed more than that in Grade 7. But, people suggest I am like him in my mannerisms and I seem to have inherited his twang as I tell my own stories. I am thankful for that. I am also happy to have his love of story and desire to make people laugh.

It started when I was a young kid. There were always visitors at our house. It was like the do-drop inn. I would perform for them, telling them jokes or doing some kind of dance or facial expression, anything that might elicit a laugh or a clap.

In elementary school, I would say funny things or do imitations to make my friends laugh. I was fortunate to have always had a sharp memory for intricate details and facts. I was blessed, or cursed, to be able to think of something off the top of my head, and to say it in a way that would make people laugh. Some of my teachers did not appreciate it, but all of my friends did.

Into my high school years and beyond, I was constantly telling stories or finding ways to give my friends a chuckle. I never thought much about why I did it, only that it seemed to make them happy and it resulted in my smiling that broad King smile.

In spite of my penchant for spinning a good yarn, I never considered myself a storyteller. I felt that was a term reserved for people like my dad and his brothers - those who understood how to construct a good story and how to deliver it for optimum effect. Storytellers were craftsmen. They were artists.

In fact, the first time I was introduced as a storyteller, I felt unworthy of the title. It was at the PEI Festival of Small Halls. I was sharing the stage with David Weale and Alan Buchanan, the deans of PEI storytelling and I certainly did not feel like I belonged. When David introduced me, I just let it roll. I received a hearty applause and the crowd was laughing. I smiled broadly and I was hooked.

Since then I have performed in many Prince Edward Island communities, telling my own stories and sharing those of my father and uncles. I have learned that most people love a good

11

story just as much as I do. Stories are special. Stories evoke an almost primal feeling. Stories are our memories and our connection to the times we loved -- a time more innocent, less complicated and revered.

I believe the true power of the story is the feeling you are left with, whether you are the listener or the teller. For me, I love when people express how much they appreciate my small role in ensuring the art of storytelling is preserved and celebrated. I love that sometimes people run into me and tell me they heard someone tell one of my stories. I love it even more when an older person tells me I am like my father.

Mostly though, I love that when I tell stories, or even just think about stories, I feel closer to my father. As if by some grand design, the stories he told - the ones that I so loved to hear - continue to keep us close, though the years are working to separate us.

That is why I decided to write this book. I wanted to preserve the stories that have brought laughter and joy to my family, my friends and all who have had the privilege to hear them. When I think of all the stories that have been forever buried with our ancestors, it makes me profoundly sad. It is my hope that these stories will continue to be heard and appreciated for many years to come, as all good stories should.

This book is a compilation of my favorite stories. Some are the stories my father told me, written as I best remember them. Some are my own stories. Some are part of local folklore. All involve special characters who deserve to be remembered and appreciated.

Good stories will always stir up a special feeling inside of you. I hope mine will do the same - and maybe leave you with a smile.

D.K.

2016

Part 1: The Stories of My Dad

PEI singer/songwriter (and my high school friend) Eddy Quinn wrote the song, "A Lot of Snows," about his late father, Merlin. It is one of my favorites. In it is a line that immediately reminds me of my own father:

"And I could smell the outdoors just like perfume off his clothes..."

My father, like most of that generation, was blue collar. All he knew was work. For almost 40 years, he sandblasted ships at the local shipyard. When he wasn't doing that six days a week, you would find him working in the woods, or picking up and hauling the town garbage. In the fall, he would sell seaweed by the truckload, popular for banking older homes in the town - anything to make a dollar.

He woke up early and worked hard until the sun went down. He only stopped to eat. Every day of his life, regardless of the season, he wore green work pants, a plaid lumberjack shirt and pair of work boots. In the dead of summer, on the hot days, he would sometimes roll up the sleeves on his shirt. But not always.

After he had supper and had wound down from the day's work, he would sit at the kitchen table, drink from a bottomless cup of tea and tell stories.

Some people say funny things and some people say things funny – my father did both.

Just about every memory I have of my father includes him being somewhere, often in front of a gaggle of people, telling a story.

When we drove in his truck, my father would tell us stories.

When we would lie in bed, my father would tell us stories.

Although most of his stories were funny, he also liked to terrify us with stories about ghosts and forerunners.

I used to think he told stories simply to entertain us, his children - which he did. But as I got older, I came to realize that he also loved to tell stories because they helped him stay connected to those parts of his life that were so important to him.

The Undertaker

When my father was 13, the Kings left Boughton Island and moved 10 miles down the coast to Georgetown, PEI. They left behind the remote Island that had no electricity, running water or indoor plumbing, and a population of 100. They arrived in the boomtown that was Georgetown in the early 1940s. Close to 1,000 people lived in this thriving metropolis. There were 18 stores, dozens of businesses and many modern luxuries. It scared the living shit out of the King family.

They never lost their affection for their Boughton Island home, but they did acclimatize nicely to the Kings County capital. It helped that many other Boughton Island families had also relocated to Georgetown. One of those families was the Gotells -- a small family for the times, consisting of four boys named Joseph, Gordon, Kimball and Basil and just one girl, Mary.

While Lionel was friends with all of the boys, he and Basil were close in age and were very good friends. Like my father, Basil had a great sense of humor, which would go on to serve him well in what was to be a challenging life. Basil had poor eyesight and would eventually go blind before the age of 45. It was a degeneration also inflicted upon an uncle on his mother's side, a man not so ceremoniously referred to as, "Blind Farrell."

Now I never knew Blind Farrell personally, but he was a familiar part of my lexicon growing up. Whenever we would see a hockey referee or baseball umpire miss a call, we would roar out, "Christ to God, Blind Farrell would have seen that." Many in

Georgetown still reference poor Mr. Farrell when similar sporting situations arise today.

It was an early summer day in Georgetown, Lionel and Basil were strolling the streets. They didn't have much to do and were trying to find a little mischief to entertain them. They were not having much luck and decided to head for a snack at the King family home on the foot of Grafton Street. It was right next door to Mae Ranton's. *(For those not old enough to remember Mae Ranton or not readily familiar with 1950s Georgetown geography, I will explain it in true Prince Edward Island fashion: The King home was located right beside where the Regal oil tanks used to be.)*

The two boys were walking down the road when they heard a voice roaring out. They turned around and saw a well-dressed man looking out the second story window of the Yorston home.

"You two lads, could you come give a man a lift?" the man asked.

Not having anything any better to do and not wanting to be impolite, the boys agreed to do so.

"Come in the front door and walk up the stairs," the man said.

The boys followed the instructions, went up through the house and happened upon the undertaker from Montague, standing over the deceased body of old Mr. Yorston. Basil was a stride behind and could not immediately see what was going on.

Neither of the boys had seen a dead body before, outside of a family wake. Lionel stopped and looked wide-eyed at the dead man. Basil finally saw what was going on and stood frozen in fear.

When telling stories in later years, Lionel would always try to insist he was quite brave and unafraid of ghosts or any of the like. In reality, he was more chicken-hearted than he would want us to believe. Basil had a similar lack of courage. When he realized there was a dead man lying on the bed, Basil made no bones about his desire to, "get the hell out" as soon as possible.

The undertaker was, of course, used to being around the dead and saw no need for anyone to be alarmed. He had little concern for the young men's fears.

"I need you fellas to hook onto him and help me put him on the board so we can carry him out to the hearse," the undertaker said nonchalantly.

The boys didn't move. They could only stare in disbelief at the dead body in their midst.

Finally, after some coaxing, they were convinced to do what was asked of them. Under more, heavier coaxing, Lionel grabbed on to the shoulders while Basil grabbed the ankles. The undertaker began to count and on three, the boys lifted the body onto the backboard. Not that the dead man would have cared, but the boys didn't let the body down as gingerly as they were planning. In fact, the body hit quite hard and as it did, a long, loud puff of wind came out.

"Huuuummmpppppphhhhhh!"

Basil and Lionel nearly fainted. The undertaker told them this was quite normal activity with a dead body but the boys were long past comfortable. They were downright antsy. They just wanted to finish the task and be on their way.

As they carried the board down through the house, my father began to sniff a strange, pungent odor. It was strong and it filled the air. It greatly concerned Lionel but since the undertaker didn't seem to take any pass of it, he just soldiered on. He looked over at Basil and took some comfort in the fact his face also appeared paralyzed in similar fear and discomfort.

After what seemed an eternity, the boys got to the back of the hearse. Not having any experience, it took them a few moments to work the body into the vehicle. The more the lads fidgeted with the body, the more the smell intensified and the more my father felt sick to his stomach.

The undertaker thanked the boys for their help and backed out of the driveway, heading for Montague to prepare the remains for the wake and funeral. Lionel and Basil just stood there. Finally, Lionel broke the silence.

"Did you get a whiff of that smell after we moved the body? Do you think they all smell like that?"

Basil looked at my father and said, "That wasn't the body Lionel. When old Mr. Yorston let go of his wind, I shit myself."

My father loved to tell us stories about growing up on Boughton Island. In his stories, the 'Island' was magical, almost mystical. Incredible, sometimes impossible events seemed to happen with surprising regularity.

The little details of his stories captivated me, such as how my father and all of his siblings always referred to their mother by her given name, Edna. They always referred to their father as Poor Daddy. No one ever knew why and we never thought to ask, but those little details helped make the stories more loveable.

As he talked, you couldn't help but appreciate the forgotten innocence of life on Boughton Island, and just how much its residents cherished the place.

The disconnect from the outside world actually helped families who lived there grow up to be more closely knit and to appreciate life's simple pleasures.

One of the pleasures most appreciated was the ability to entertain one another, and yourself, by creating prose, poetry or stories. The good stories were the ones that made others laugh or, in the case of ghost stories, induced terror.

My father was great at terrifying us. He would wait until we were in bed, turn down the lights, lower his voice to just beyond a whisper and tell us about his many meetings with ghosts, forerunners, the supernatural and the unexplained. Sometimes he would grab us as he delivered the punch line.

We loved it. Though frozen with fear, the exhilaration was addictive and we would ask him to tell us more. We must have heard his stories hundreds of times, but they never failed to scare the bejesus out of us and we loved them more each time we heard them.

One night, after he had told us his regular set of ghost stories, I asked my father to tell us one we had never heard before. He grew silent. He stayed that way for what seemed like an eternity.

Finally, he lowered his voice and began.

A Visit from Nathan Allen?

I left school in the spring just before the end of Grade 4. On Boughton Island, work took priority over everythin', includin' education. Not that I minded - I was able to write my name and read some. I figured that was about what I needed to make my way.

Every spring, the lobster canneries would start up on the Island. I remember at its peak there were over a dozen canneries. Workers would come from as far as Newport, Georgetown, Launchin', Sturgeon, Lower Montague and other places. They would stay for the spring and can the lobsters that were being trapped just off the shore.

Jeez, the ol' Island would just be jumpin'. The population would more than double and there were plenty of jobs for young gaffers like me to make a few dollars.

I was livin' at home. Poor Daddy fished and farmed. When the Liberals were in Ottawa, he got the job of markin' the ice with brush to show the locals and visitors the safest path between the Island and Launchin'. It wasn't a big government job, but he appreciated it. Poor Daddy was a good worker and Lord Jesus he was hard. They didn't mess with Dan King let me tell yas that!

My mother Edna was sickly and never well. She suffered from epilepsy and often took fits. Her mother, my grandmother, Fanny Allen, lived with us and she looked after the home chores. She was a lovely lady - kind to a fault. I figured the bit of money I would make in the spring would help pay for some of the winter's supplies we bought on tack at Jim Hayter's store in Launchin'.

My job was easy. I would remove the lobster crates from the factory and stack them five-high for the fishermen to use the next day. There was a bit of luggin' to it, but nothin' I couldn't handle. And then when the cannin' was done for the day, I would work with the cleanin' crew to get it all ready for the next day.

My work would finish about 9:30 in the evenin'. I would warsh up and make my way up the path to home. I suppose it was about 1500 feet or so. Between the factory and home was the little hut that belonged to my uncle, Nathan Allen. He was my mother's brother.

Nathan Allen was a bachelor. Now, he was a nice fella but many would call him a bit of a queer duck. And he was a terrible moody bugger. If the moon was full, it was likely he wouldn't talk to you at all. Not even a grunt. He'd just sit in the rockin' chair next to the wood stove and stare right past ya.

I was used to this of course. It didn't bother me none at all. Every day I would stop in to visit with him, we would have a cup of tea and a biscuit perhaps. I would ask him questions about the size of lobster hauls that day or if Frank McCormack's cow had calved. If he was in the mood he would answer and if he wasn't, he wouldn't. That's kind of how it all went with him.

Every night on the way home, I would stop in for a visit. He would be sitting in the chair, sometimes the tea would be on and I would pour us a cup. If the teapot was empty, I'd brew a batch. I wouldn't stay longer than 10 or 15 minutes, even shorter if he wasn't in the talkin' frame of mind.

This one evening, the cannin' went longer than normal. It was half past ten or so before I got clear and made my way up home. I stopped in to see Nathan. I knew he was still up because I could see the lantern burnin' through the window. There he was, sittin' in the chair, just like I'd seen him a thousand times.

I put the teapot on, fetched us a biscuit that my grandmother Fanny Allen would have made, and sat down. I asked him a few questions. He said nothin'. He didn't seem much to be in the talkin' mood. He just sat there. Wasn't so much lookin' past me as much as he was lookin' through me. He never even made a grunt.

I put a cup of tea in front of him, but he didn't bother with it. It was late after all and he was likely all tea'd out. After a few more minutes and a bunch of questions that were left unanswered, I cleared the teacups and bid him goodbye. I made my way up the path for home.

When I got home, poor Daddy was sitting in the kitchen.

"Where the hell have you been boy?" he asked me sternly. I told him that work went a bit later than normal and I had just stopped in for a cup of tea with Nathan Allen.

Poor Daddy's face went blank.

"You just had tea with Nathan Allen?" he asked.

I was perplexed. Poor Daddy knew I would never happen by Nathan Allen's without going in for a visit. It just wouldn't be proper. I told him that Nathan was in one of those queer moods and didn't have much to say tonight. In fact, I found him more distant than normal.

Poor Daddy stood up. His face was as white as snow. I'd never seen him look so ashen. It was the first time I remember him lookin' afraid.

"Lionel dear," he said. "You couldn't have had tea with Nathan Allen this evening. They found him dead this mornin'."

I often talk with my sisters and brothers about dad's stories and inevitably, the discussion will turn to all-time favorites. He told us so many tales, it is hard to choose, but one we all remember and appreciate is the one he always called, The Ice Cakes.

There were eight kids in our family, stretched over 20 years, and we lived in a one-and-a-half story house with three small bedrooms. My oldest brother, Benji, left for college and never permanently moved back. Lloydie, second oldest, slept on the couch. Peggy and Pammy shared a room and for reasons we cannot explain, brother Mark had his own bed. My sister Toby and I shared a bed at the foot of our parent's bed. The youngest, Susie, slept with Mom and Dad. If it was a tight fit, we never really noticed.

At bedtime, we would snuggle in and those of us in mom and dad's room would beg for a couple of stories before going to sleep. The room would be dark and all you could see were two little orange dots - both mom and dad liked to smoke before going to sleep! Dad would pretend not to know any stories at first, but then he would open up. After a couple of Boughton Island stories, we would beg for, The Ice Cakes.

The Ice Cakes

Growing up on Boughton Island, we didn't leave the Island much - only when we needed supplies from Jim Hayter's store in Launchin'.

We could row a skiff across the channel to Launchin' most of the year. In the winter, we'd have wait for the ice to freeze and when it did, Poor Daddy would mark a safe path with fir boughs wide enough for a horse and sleigh.

Mostly, Poor Daddy would go himself, especially when the channel was open, so he could put more supplies in the skiff. The odd time in winter, when there was room, he'd take one of us with him. It was a big treat to get to Launchin', let me tell ya. There was a great big glass jar full to the top with black licorice and as sure as I am layin' here, it was the sweetest thing I ever smelled.

Winter stayed real late this one year, and it was real funny weather. Spring was tryin' to get here but there was still lots of snow, then it would mild right up one night, and cool down the next. The ice wasn't gone, but it wasn't near thick enough to run a horse and sleigh over. And, of course, there was too much ice for a wooden skiff.

We were gettin' down pretty good on supplies and my grandmother, Fanny Allen, was anxious for the ice to clear enough so Poor Daddy could get across the channel. All it would take would be a good day's wind or two from the north to clear the channel out. But Poor Daddy was smart. He knew the channel ran hard and quick. If the wind turned and blew out of the south, the channel would fill back in.

We didn't have a radio or nothin' then sayin' the weather. Poor Daddy tried his best to gauge the situation and finally decided he would take the walk across the ice for supplies. After much convincin' he agreed to take my brother Donald with him for company.

We didn't have phones or lights either, but the old people were terrible resourceful. They worked out a way to communicate across the channel to let people know they were safe. At dark, if you weren't goin' to get back to the Island you could go down to the shore, light a lantern and wave it for others to see. Someone on the Island shore would do the same and everyone could rest easy knowin' all was safe.

Poor Daddy and Donald made it across the channel without much trouble and got to Jim Hayters' about half past six. Jim was surprised to see them and told them they were foolish to have tried such a voyage this time of year. Jim's wife got them some tea and biscuits for a little snack and after a time, they set off for the shore and the trip back.

Jeez, when they got down to the beach, the wind had shifted and all the ice was gone. The channel was as clear as a bell. Poor Daddy and Donald walked back up to the store. They told Jim about the channel and asked if he had skiff they could use to get home.

Now Jim Hayter had known Poor Daddy his whole life and would never not do a turn for him if he needed it. But, Jim didn't have a skiff. His neighbour up the road, William Christian, had one. Jim wasn't too keen on seeing two lads head across that tricky channel, particularly after dark in this funny spring. He tried to convince them to spend the night, but Poor Daddy was wantin' to get back to the Island. He and Donald set off for William Christian's.

William was no more keen on seeing the Kings row across the channel than Jim was, but when Poor Daddy asked him the second time, William knew there was no stoppin' him. Poor Daddy hooked on the skiff and carried it to the shore. It was a good size skiff but Poor Daddy was fearful strong. He carried it like it was nothin'. Donald drug the sled with the supplies.

When they got back to the shore, the wind had shifted again and it looked like some of the ice was makin' its way back into the channel. Donald lit the lantern and waved it five or six times and blew it out. A few minutes later they could see the lantern on the other shore wavin'. They headed back up the way to Jim Hayter's, who was happy to put them up for the night.

The next morning, not long before sun up, there was a knock on the door at Jim Hayter's store. Jim opened the door and there was William Christian. He was as white as a sheet.

He says, "Jim, Dan King and his son were drowned last night. They borrowed my skiff. I didn't want to give it to them but he insisted. The wind changed and the channel is packed with ice. Gosh darn it Jim, the skiff warshed back ashore but they are nowhere to be seen. I shouldn't have given them that skiff."

Just then, Poor Daddy and Donald came down the stairs. At first, William thought he saw two ghosts. Once he realized they were alive and well, he was some happy to see them! He thanked Jim for holdin' them up for the night.

Poor Daddy and Donald hooked on to the sleigh and they walked across the ice. They got home as safe as a church. And, that's the story called, *The Ice Cakes!*

My dad always believed in the afterlife and told many stories in which he interacted with ghosts. He would tell of being visited in his sleep by friends who had long passed on. I always kind of thought he was full of crap – that these stories were just more foolish attempts to scare us. I am not so sure anymore.

I awoke one morning, about four years ago, with a crystal-clear memory in my head. It was not the first time I had dreamed of my father or the stories he had told - it happens often - but this time was different. This dream was much more vivid and it felt very real.

In the dream, my dad pulled up a chair beside my bed and told me a story. When I awoke, I called my brother Mark, told him the story and asked if he remembered hearing it. He did not. Then I called my mother and asked the same, she did not recall the story either, but confirmed the details and names were familiar and accurate.

Was it my subconscious? Perhaps. Was it a real visit from my long-dead father? I suppose I will never know. But, if it was, I hope he returns again soon. With more great stories like this one he told me that night in my dream.

The Corn Broom

In the 1950s, Georgetown was in need of a new rink. Many community-minded individuals figured the time was right to build something that would last, and would do the town proud.

A similar undertaking in neighboring Montague a few years earlier resulted in the formation of a *Community Welfare League* -- a group formed by residents, local merchants and town officials to oversee the planning, fundraising and construction.

Montague had more merchants and entrepreneurs than Georgetown, of course. Montague also enjoyed a reputation of being a community that could put petty differences aside and work together for the greater good. This was not something the residents of the Kings County capital could be easily accused of.

In spite of this, it was determined that Georgetown would follow Montague's lead and strike its own *Community Welfare League*, which would eventually lead to the construction of a new hockey rink for the town. (Aside from this story, my father penned a famous poem about this challenging undertaking called *The Georgetown Rink*, which can be seen in Part 2 of this book.)

Percy Boudreault was asked, and accepted, the role of chair of the founding meetings. Everyone just called him Perce. He was an entrepreneur who owned a meat store in the town. He was street-smart and patient with crowds. He also had a sharp wit and cutting tongue. He was not hesitant to use either.

The first meeting began at the town hall with very good crowds participating. People were engaged in the process. People offered up their thoughts and ideas as to what the rink should look like or what would be the best way to go about raising the money needed to make it happen.

About 45 minutes into the meeting, Joe Johnson entered the room. Joe was well thought of in the community, but he was also known for having a bit of a stubborn streak. While he would do anything for a friend or neighbour, things seemed to go along best if being done Joe's way.

Joe immediately began to ask questions about what he had missed, who said what, and then he began to offer his thoughts and opinions. It would take another 40 minutes for Perce to get the meeting back on schedule.

Community meetings were held weekly and, as is often the case in Georgetown, they took on a consistent tone. Things would start smoothly with the agenda closely adhered to, until the 45-minute mark when Joe would arrive, begin to ask questions and rehash the meeting. It would take another 40 minutes for Perce to get the meetings back on the rails.

Now, this greatly frustrated Perce, but he did not want to criticize Joe. Perce knew Joe's carpentry skills would be crucial to the eventual construction of the new facility. He also knew that Joe just wanted a good finished product.

The next meeting was 45 minutes in, and just like clockwork, Joe arrived. As he reached for a vacant chair near the table, Perce got up and grabbed the corn broom leaning against the wall. He passed it to Waldron Lavers and said, "you can put that broom away now Waldron."

Waldron, somewhat perplexed, grabbed the broom and headed for the storage closet. Joe had an inquiring mind and asked "Perce, what were yas doing with the broom?"

Perce replied tersely.

"That's what we were tripping over until you got here!"

Part 2: The Boughton Island Poets' Society

Growing up in the early 1900s, on a remote Island, off the coast of a small Island in the Atlantic Ocean provided a unique and sheltered upbringing for my father and his siblings.

Rather than loathe the difficulties and challenges, the Kings embraced their island lifestyle and often viewed their life on Boughton Island with blessed enchantment. Though they moved away at a young age, the Kings remained enthralled and immersed in the legend of Boughton Island. They recalled their life there with pride, and forever remained nostalgic about their home.

I grew up listening to, and later telling, stories about Head's Pond, Ball's Rock and countless other landmarks the island boasted - landmarks I have only seen through the eyes of my father's imagination. As I write, I feel the same nostalgia.

Though the King clan would spend their days on the island immersed in the chores of the mixed-farm and fishing lifestyle of their folks, there was a good deal of down time. With little connection to the outside world, the Kings and the other residents of Boughton Island would entertain themselves by writing poems, creating and telling stories and generally just trying to outdo one another. It was friendly, but competitive, and so entertaining.

Often, small, remote islands are remembered for buried treasures. I believe the bounty of the treasure of Boughton Island was the gift of good storytelling. It was a skill the island residents embraced and one they spent their lives honing -- and the world is better for it.

Many of the descendants of the families that lived on Boughton Island at the time are, today, gifted storytellers in their own right. The Gotells, the Allens, the Kings and many others share a dry wit, with the ability to stretch the truth or turn a phrase that, as it turns out, is quintessentially Boughton Island. I am so honored to be one of them.

Fair Boughton Isle
By John (Jack) C. King

There's a dear Isle on earth
It's the isle of my birth
In my memory it ever holds dear

T'was on old Boughton Isle
That the sun on me smiled
And I spent happy childhood days there

But as the years they rolled by
Many changes occurred
And I left that dear isle by the sea

Now I am sitting and thinking
And thoughts wander back
To the Isle that was Heaven to me

Now the sons and the daughters
Of ol' Boughton Isle
'Tis happy and proud they should be

To claim for their birth
That garden on earth
That beautiful isle by the sea

Perhaps in death's slumber
I'll see in my dreams
Your dew diamond meadows
Your bright shining streams

And faces of loved ones
We've lost for a time
Who once dwelt with me

On this beautiful Isle.

Uncle Jack's Wedding Toast
By John (Jack) C. King

Strange, electrical appliances
Have super-ceded steam.
And the oblong sailing vessel
Is just an antiquated dream

Automobiles have been replaced
By horse drawn carriages for the rich
And, women still wear silk hosiery
Yet they never knit a stitch

And that belly ache we used to have
Is called appendix now
And yes we still eat dairy butter
But it's never seen a cow

Now, progress is our motto
Modern times they are here to stay
But, thank GOD they still make babies
In that same, old fashioned way!

(After a hearty applause and laughter, he'd continue)

I wish you health
I wish you wealth
I wish you love in great store
I wish you twins at every birth
How could I wish you more?

The Georgetown Rink
By Lionel King

There's a country town called Georgetown
On fair Prince Edward's Isle.
It's composed of different kinds of folks
Whose actions make you smile.

There's French and English and some Scots
We have the Irish too.
And in your walk around this town,
You will meet up with a Jew.

There's guys who've lived here all their lives,
They're simply in a rut.
Cause all they do from morn' 'til night,
Is sit around their hut.

They started here just lately,
To form a welfare league.
They copied this from Montague,
A noble act indeed.

And first the leader started,
A guy of brawn and brain.
He's known to each and everyone
As the guy called Binx MacLean.

First that wonder started,
And still that wonder grew.
How one small head just such as his,
Could carry all he knew.

And then they went to Boudreault,
Another of this kind.
He answers yes with that loud laugh,
So speaks the vacant mind.

And then they went to Waldron Lavers,
A wizard at the law.
He formed up the agreement,
The best you ever saw.

They say he is peculiar,
According to his story.
He praised the Grits from morn to night,
But, still he voted Tory.

And then they went to Johnson,
A man with inside news.
If you would watch his actions,
You would certainly be amused.

First, he shrugged his shoulders,
Then chucked out his chest.
He blew smoke from a cheap cigar,
And said, "I'll join the rest."

Then they went to Howard Mac,
A man of great renown.
He used to run a corner store,
But he had to close it down.

He's a man of great importance,
He's a man among all men.
But he'll say that three and two are six,
And five and four make ten.

Then they went to Soloman.
They placed him at the top,
He certainly knows his business,
He runs a barber shop.

He's nigh onto 60 years,
Behind a barber's sink.
But he awoke just recently,
To build the boys a rink.

Now somewhere in the book it reads
If I am not a simp.
That if you live among the lame,
You will wind up with a limp.

And, further in that book it reads,
We are all ordained to die.
And, it is there we will meet our maker,
Away up there on high.

And, when he passes judgement day,
It's then he'll make you think,
Because he will say, "Depart from me,
You built the Georgetown Rink!"

The Colorful Toast
By Lionel King

Here's to the girl
With the little red shoes
She likes her cigarettes
And she likes her booze
She may have lost her cherry
But that is not a sin
For she still has the box
That her cherry came in!

Helping Her Soldier Come Home
By Donald C. King aged 12 (1940)

There's a little girl that's waiting for her noble soldier lad
He has left and gone to England, leaves her lonely, blue and sad
Now this little girl that's waiting, tried to do her duty home
She is working in a war plant, trying to help her soldier home
When his furlough it is granted, how he wishes he was home
For to see his dear old mother and the girl he left alone
When this cruel war is over and the soldiers leave for home
There'll be some of them that's missing left to seek a better home

Grandmother's funeral song
By Donald C. King

Now friends if you listen I'll tell you a song
About Boughton Island the place I was born
Surrounded by the water, as you see by the name
Where one's heart sometimes longs to be back again

We lived in the center, yet close to the shore
Just open the window and hear the surf roar
As kids few in numbers, we had lots of fun
And the old folks joined in when their day's work was done

Away from the rat race, we never knew crime
There were things we were short of, but one was not time
We had time for pleasure, we found time for fun
And always the time when the work must be done

To the oldest one born there, I cannot go back
But the oldest still living with us, we call him Joe Mac
Joe left the Island for the first Great World War
While Islanders' hearts were left heavy and sore

But after four years of warfare and strain
Joe returned to the Island again
Now living in Cardigan some 90 years young
He's the one left to say how this song should be sung

For this was in mother and grandmother's day
Born Boughton Islanders, gone by the way
A funeral like grandmother's you don't see today
For it was a fishing boat that took her away

Sixteen fishing boats all in a line
And I now speak from memory though small at the time
From the Island to Annandale that was the route
The black horse and hearse wagon replaced by the boat

But I'm wondering if people are as happy today
As they were in those days of old
If you could ask this to people one hundred years back
The answer would surely be no

We oft times have said they had nothing to do
We said they had nowhere to go
But one of the old people's favorite sayings
"you only shall reap what you sow"

Some outdoor sports that we're doing today
They did them, but in different ways
They climbed a hill to the top to coast down
While we sit in a motoring sleigh

They made their own songs, the most of them long
In each one a story was told
To this present day we still sing their songs
Their stories, they never grow old.

The Merchant named Jim
By Donald C. King

They say Jim Hayter is leaving
He's going a long way from here
Although he is running a good business
To Souris his passage will steer

In two month's time he is leaving
His house he is going to sell
To a man by the name of Nat Taylor
In Sturgeon he used to dwell

The Island folks say they will miss him
Where they always bought many's a thing
But if he says he is going
There's no use of trying to stop him

The Launching folks are regretting
The day when they will lose him
For they did a lot of their shopping
With the merchant who's named was called Jim

But now my story is ending
It's a story that's short but true
So long to you, Mr Hayter
And the very best of luck to you.

Growing up, we spent a great deal of time at my uncle Donald's place. As my father was a habitual visitor, a frequent popper-inner with his family and friends, we would often have to entertain ourselves as Dad shared a conversation over a cup of tea with uncle Donald.

My father and his brother Jack were talented and accomplished storytellers, but they always played second fiddle to uncle Donald, who was as good or better than any teller I have heard. Uncle Donald was a presence. He had confidence, lively eyes, a sly grin, his voice was smothered with a thick, Island-ized twang and he had a unique way of talking out of the bottom corner of his mouth. All of this made his stories

authentic, and when it was combined with his dry wit and sharp tongue,
the end result was pure magic. He was brilliantly funny.

Sage Advice from Uncle Donald

As I grew up, I was fortunate to become quite close with my uncle Donald. I think it was because I developed a greater appreciation for the craft of storytelling, and had a deep admiration of his clever mind for stories. I also believe he appreciated that I had some of the King wit and devilishness, and seldom hesitated to use either.

I am glad we had the chance to become close, and as I pursue storytelling in more dedicated fashion, I find myself thinking that uncle Donald would be proud. I have fond memories of the time we spent together.

One time when I was working as a newspaper reporter covering the PEI Legislature, I took him with me to watch Question Period at historic Province House. Uncle Donald was a political animal and keen observer of the news. When I picked him up, he was dressed in a suit jacket and tie. I joked that we were only going to watch the proceedings, not participate. He smiled.

There is a great tradition before Question Period when each politician stands and welcomes various special guests in attendance. Many of the eastern PEI MLAs stood and welcomed Donald, complimenting him on his career with CN Marine and in the lobster fishery. But, most of all, he was recognized and appreciated for being a great spinner of stories and poems.

Uncle Donald didn't say much at the time, but I could tell by his beaming smile that he was proud. And, that he was grateful that I had taken him into the proceedings. We had a wonderful day.

About a year later, I was to be married in Summerside. Prior to the ceremony beginning, I was waiting in a small room at the back of the Anglican church with my best man Derek Johnson. We were making small talk and trying not to be too nervous about the pending ceremony. Suddenly, the door opened and uncle Donald walked in. He quickly extended his hand of congratulations.

We chatted for a few minutes, but it became apparent that Donald had more than simple pleasantries on his mind. He pulled up a chair and sat down, looked down at the floor and gave his head a twist to the side. He had something important he wanted to say.

"Now boy, your father isn't here today and he's a great miss. He'd be awfully proud of you if he was here," uncle Donald told me.

It meant a lot to me to hear that. I looked away and tried hard to swallow the big lump in my throat that had suddenly appeared. After a quiet moment, he reached into his jacket pocket and pulled out a bottle of Lamb's rum, held it out in front of me and encouraged me to take a drink. I took a small sip.

"Jeez, boy, take a good pull out of that to calm your nerves."

I did as I was instructed then I passed the bottle to Derek, who took a big drink before handing it back to uncle Donald. He took a substantial drink before returning the bottle to his jacket. Then, he said it was the proper time for some father to son advice about the wedding and married life in general.

"If poor Lionel was here, he would be telling you, so I guess will tell you in his place," uncle Donald said.

"You are going to be up on the altar and the whole crowd is going to be staring at you. The Minister is going to going through his spiel and even though you are going to be doing your best to concentrate on that, you are going to be distracted by a rather loud slappin' sound."

Puzzled, I looked at him.

"A slapping sound? What kind of slap do you mean?"

Uncle Donald didn't answer my question, he just continued on, telling me to do my very best to ignore the sound, to just stay focused on the task at hand. He said it would all be over soon enough.

I told him that I would do my best, but I was perplexed by this slapping sound and what it might be.

"So, this slapping sound, what do you suppose it is," I asked.

Uncle Donald twisted his head, smiled that sly grin and started to speak out of the bottom corner of his mouth as only uncle Donald could.

"Son, that's her legs closing shut!"

The stories, poems and songs in this chapter by Donald C. King were first published in his book: Memories of Boughton Island, published in 2005. The stories are used with his family's permission.

Part 3: The King Homestead

My parents moved to an old house on the Kayes Road in Georgetown Royalty when I was two years old. The "Royalty" is about three miles outside of greater, downtown, metropolitan Georgetown (population 730).

The one-and-a-half story farmhouse was rundown and not nearly big enough for the family of 10 that would call it home. Still, it was much larger than the little hut of a spot we left on Glenelg Street in Georgetown.

Dad said he took one look at the house and knew it had personality. Others didn't share the sentiment. Dad would tell us that friends and family took bets on whether the family would starve or freeze to death that first winter. Thankfully neither happened.

The King homestead was heaven to us. We were crammed into bedrooms and beds, but nobody seemed to mind. Yes, we fought and argued, but we almost always enjoyed each other's company and made the best of what we had. I suspect it is the main reason why our family remains so close-knit today. We still enjoy each other's company and we always make the best of the time we have together.

Our house was the place where friends and neighbours were always welcome. No one knocked on the door or took their boots off before entering. Guests just came in and made themselves at home. They would find a seat around the kitchen table, where a card game or a topical discussion, sometimes both, would take place. The stories poured out almost as fast as the tea.

It never looked like it on the inside, or the outside, but our home was as magical as the Disney castle. We were given the time and space to be creative, to entertain, to find our talents and to appreciate others. We were surrounded by love and grew up immersed in great debates, featuring witty and sharp tongues that brought about more laughs than anger. It was beautiful in more ways than I could begin to explain.

When we first moved there, the Kayes Road had no pavement. The spring and fall meant parking at the foot of the road, on Highway 3 and hoofing it to the house. Only a fool would live there, people would tell my dad. Today, some of the best and most expensive properties in the area are located along the Brudenell River on the Kayes Road. Turns out, only a fool would not want to live there now.

My brother Benji and I still own the house. I try to get down as often as I can in the summer. It is the place I feel most grounded. It is the place I feel most connected to my father and my family. It is heaven. It is home. And, it still has personality!

The Teapot

The lifeblood of our house in Georgetown Royalty flowed from a bottomless teapot.

Our parents could barely function without first coming to grips with the status of the teapot.

"Is the teapot on?"

"Put the teapot on."

"Take the teapot off."

"Fill the teapot up."

"Add a bag to the teapot."

My mother would seldom get out of bed in the morning without a loving roar downstairs, "Dad, do you have the teapot on?"

He'd chuckle to himself, yell back with a positive, "Well, I'd imagine," and it wasn't long before mother would make her way from the second floor to start her day. As he had done an hour or so earlier, she'd first settle at the kitchen table with a cup of tea and a home-rolled smoke. "A whore's breakfast," Dad called it.

The first tea of the day was a fresh pot of water with three or four tea bags. We had a glass teapot, with a steel band wrapped around the middle. If you took a few minutes and scrubbed really hard, you could roughly make out the "stainless steel" insignia on the side, and though it was glass, you couldn't see through it. It was never out of service long enough to wash therefore it got only an occasional rinse at the beginning of each day.

As the day progressed, more water was added, along with a tea bag or two. Come supper time there would be as many as twelve bags in the pot and the tea was so strong you could float a potato in it. Strong tea can be a bit much for the faint of heart. Not so at our place. If you found the tea too strong, the simple remedy was just to add more milk.

My folks and the regular visitors to our home drank their tea with canned milk - Carnation 2%. Dad would punch a hole in either side with a steak knife then pry one of the holes open wider than the other. The can would go back in the fridge until the next time it was needed, and when it came out again, if part of the previous pour had curdled enough to close the hole over, Mom would simply dab her tongue a couple of times over the hardened milk to free it.

For as long as I can remember that was how they drank tea: fill the cup two-thirds to the top with tea as black as coal, grab the can of milk from the fridge and give the hardened curd a hearty lick or two, add as much milk as the cup would hold, and drink. And drink, and drink, and drink.

Red Rose was the tea of choice. There may have been a time or two when King Cole was used, but only during rare interruptions in the MacConnell's Clover Farm supply chain. I sometimes saw commercials on television for Tetley tea, but for the life of me, I cannot recall a time when a box of Tetley found its way into our house.

Ours was a humble home, small and quaint with nothing fancy of any kind inside. As was the case with most rural Island abodes, what it lacked in style it more than made up for in character and hospitality. In those days, before instant communication devices, or even cable television, the visit was our primary form of entertainment. Friends and family stopped by so often I was hard-pressed to distinguish between the two.

Visits would involve funny stories, vicious arguments over politics and hockey, the latest and juiciest local gossip as well as whatever might have headlined the suppertime news. An ultra-competitive game of 45s for quarters would often break out. They'd bicker and argue, thump the table for a hard-earned "trick" and curse each other sideways if the ace of hearts was inadvertently trumped with the five or jack.

Whatever would occur, the events of the night were fuelled by the teapot. Visitors always left happy, and they always came back for more tea.

I am quite certain when the teapot was purchased there was a glass top for it. But, I don't ever remember seeing it. Perhaps it was smashed during a hasty pour, not having been properly fastened. And, it was fitting I suppose. There was no bottom to the teapot, why would it need a top?

When I was a kid, I would often follow my dad around, as kids are wont to do. Often, when he was going somewhere he would ask me to go with him. He'd always say, "We are going on a little adventure."

It was a fitting term because often our little trips ended up being memorable adventures or almost always involved some incredible event that still causes me to smile and shake my head, all these years later.

The things I do with my kids today, sadly, are far from the types of adventures I had with my father. Those were the greatest days of my life.

The Hateful Bull

I have long observed that farmers are a unique breed. There is an eternal optimism to a farmer, particularly when life has beaten him down and when there is absolutely no reason for it. My father never told me much about his dreams, but if I had to guess, I would say he always wanted to be a farmer. He had the unbridled optimism to be a damn good farmer, but as much as he planned and as hard as he tried, he never seemed to be able to pull it off.

In Georgetown Royalty, we had what would best be described as a mixed hobby farm. "Mixed," because it had a collection of chickens, pigs, a small garden and sometimes a cow. "Hobby," because he spent almost every minute of his spare time at it and never made a single, red copper.

To try to make ends meet and feed eight kids, my father worked as a sandblaster at the Georgetown Shipyard. He worked their eight hours a day, six days a week for almost 40 years. And, he hated every single second of it. One evening he came home for supper and he had a big smile on his face. As he was eating, he told me that we were going on a little adventure. When I asked where we were going, his answer was short, proud and confident.

"We're getting a bull."

See, my father had come up with a new grand scheme. He was going to buy a calf, raise it for two years and then take it into the beef sale in Charlottetown. The outcome of this scheme was never in doubt.

"We'll make a clean fortune," he proclaimed.

As supper finished, my father and I jumped into my brother Lloyd's 1974 Monte Carlo. The car had more square footage than our house. You could fit half of Georgetown in it. It had leather bucket seats that turned all the way around and it was my brother's prized possession. It burned oil like you wouldn't believe and as it sailed down the road, it left a bluish, smokey plume in its wake. One time Lloyd went to Lumpy's Garage in Cardigan and told the gas attendant, "Fill 'er up with oil and check the gas." But, she was a beauty if there ever was one.

Dad told Lloyd to head for Philip MacEachern's farm in Cardross, just outside of Cardigan. When we got there, Philip greeted us with a smile and a handshake. He was a giant of a man, but very kind and gentle. We exchanged pleasantries and he showed dad around the farm. Dad stopped to admire the cattle and the tractor. He even asked if the posts in the new pole barn were hemlock or spruce. After a while, Philip pointed out the calf and my father clapped his hands with excitement. It was a dandy.

Dad paid Philip $40 for the calf as I recall. After he put the money in his overalls, Philip grabbed a burlap feed bag, put it over the calf's head, picked him up like he was a newborn baby and put him in the trunk of the Monte Carlo. Dad and Phillip thought this was great. Lloyd wasn't so keen on it, nor was the calf as it turned out.

The calf kicked, thrashed and bawled all the way to Georgetown. When Dad opened the trunk to retrieve him, all you could see and smell was cow dung. The calf had the scours and he was covered from hoof to head in brown, runny shit. Lloyd was horrified, but Dad never batted an eye. He grabbed the calf and carried him straight to the barn.

My father's plan was in full bloom. He was convinced nothing could go wrong.

The trip in the trunk of the car seemed to have a profound effect on the animal, and not in a positive way. He developed a horrible, sour, hateful and aggressive disposition. And, he maintained it for his whole life. He could best be described as a hateful, no-good bastard to be around. Every time dad would go to feed it, the calf would run at him and try to gore him - twice a day, every day, for two years. Dad, ever the optimist, seemed to think that was fine.

"The wild ones make for better steak," he told me.

I'm not sure if science backs up the belief, but it seemed to make sense at the time.

After 18 months, the animal had grown into quite a beast, or so it seemed to us as he paraded in the small field, near the tiny barn in our backyard. It was decided: the sale was upon us and it was time for dad to cash in.

Dad could always see things play out in his mind and he had no trouble sharing his thoughts with us. "Jesus," he'd say, "this fellow will be something. He will fetch a tremendous price."

As we walked to the barn, he boasted he even figured he'd make enough cash to get me a bike at Handy Andy's in Montague. Things were working out just great for the Kings.

My father, along with his friends Mike Steele and Dennis Clory came together to load the bull into the homemade cattle box on the back of the truck. They put a lasso rope around the animal's neck which Clory, the youngest and the strongest, was going to pull on. Steele was given a little switch and told to give the bull a snap on the hind end every now and then to encourage him along. Dad was overseeing from behind and when the time was right, he would close and lock the cattle box.

Clory reefed hard on the rope. The bull never moved. Steele gave him a snap with the switch. Still the bull held his ground. Clory put the rope around a fence post for added leverage and began to pull with all his might. Steele was hitting the bull repeatedly. Finally, the bull started to move, but only his head. It quickly became apparent they had tied a slip knot on the rope and the bull's wind was being choked off. At one point, the bull's front legs gave out and he went down in a heap.

Steele rushed over to loosen the knot just as Clory gave up a little slack on the rope. This was just enough for the bull to get a breath of air and when he did, he jumped to his feet and took off on the dead run, pulling the rope out of Clory's hands. The bull had fixed its eyes on Steele, who was also on the dead run - for his life!

Steele dove behind the big oak tree just as the bull was going to put the horns to him. There is still a long deep scar on the oak tree today.

Steele collected himself. Clory got a hold of the rope and after a colossal battle that would rival Ali-Frazier, they somehow managed to get the animal loaded. It was time for our adventure to Charlottetown.

The bull was in no better trim when we landed at the sale but some hired guns helped us get him off and penned. The real genius of my father's plan could now be set in motion. He and Steele were going to walk around the sale, talking to every person there about this tremendous animal they had seen in the barn. They were to talk the bull up and not let on he belonged to them. Once they got the buzz going, there would be a bidding war and the payoff would be even greater.

The sale started and the animals were paraded into the sale ring, one at a time. I remember thinking that the first animals seemed much bigger, tamer and cleaner than our guy. But what did I know? Dad was confident and all I cared about was getting a bike.

The sale was about two hours old. Dad kept building the case for the prized animal from Georgetown with all who would listen. But, there was no sign of our hateful bull and this was concerning to Dad. He pulled Steele aside and whispered for him to, "Go see if the bastard ran away."

Steele did as he was asked and quickly reported back that our bull was in the pen and that he must be coming soon. The animals continued to be paraded in and sold. The sale was more than three hours old now and the crowd was much thinner than it had been at the start. Dad justified it by suggesting the tire kickers went home and it was just the serious bidders left. Apparently, that was good news for us.

The sale broke for 10 minutes and when it resumed, the auctioneer began selling pitchforks, wheelbarrows, wagon wheels and various other pieces of light farm equipment. The crowd continued to thin out. At just past the four-hour mark, we could see the shadow of an animal in the runway. Dad looked around. There were about four other people left in the sale building: a 90-year-old woman in a wheel chair who was facing the exit, her back to the sale ring and three old farmers sitting down in the corner. They were laughing and telling stories. One of them was cleaning his ear with his truck key.

Finally, our hateful bull had arrived. One farmhand was pulling on the rope with all his might, while another was standing behind the animal, doing everything short of beating it senseless with a corn broom.

Our bull was introduced. He had 14-inch curly horns and 18 months worth of matted cow shit all over him. He didn't look quite as big in the sale ring as he did back home.

After what seemed like eternity and a colossal battle that would rival Ali-Frazier 2, the animal was in the ring. The hateful bull took three steps forward, turned all the way around, tilted his head sideways, looked right up into the stands, directly at my father and let out a deep, long MOOOOOOOOOOOOOOOOOOOO!

Dad got $50 for him.

A common hypothetical question often asked is, "If you were stranded on a deserted Island, what would you wish for?" For me, that answer is simple. I would wish for my brother Benji. My oldest brother is equal parts resourceful, dependable, determined, rustically-innovative and stubborn. I know he would find a way for us to survive and thrive on said island and eventually find a way home. He was my first hero. He is still my biggest hero.

Everybody needs a Benji!

Everybody needs a Benji. He is the brother who will never say no to you. He is the brother who will work from start to finish on a project with you and not charge you a penny. He is the brother whose door is always open, where you never have to knock, who would do anything in the world for his family. He is the epitome of kindness.

Benji was the first born in our family. There are 20 years between he and my youngest sister, Susan. When Benji was finishing high school, the younger Kings were just getting on the go. With that kind of age gap between siblings, it can be hard to develop or maintain a close connection, but Benji made the time and effort to ensure that didn't happen with us.

My earliest memories of Benji are looking at a plethora of ribbons and medals he had accumulated as one of the top sprinters for his age group, in Prince Edward Island. On the road next to the King Homestead, Benji buried two white poles, 100 meters apart. Here, he would don his sprinter's spikes and run for what seemed like hours. He was as fast as a scalded cat.

After playing football in high school, Benji attended Acadia University in Wolfville, NS and tried out for the college football team. He was only about 5'6", 145 pounds, but he was determined, he worked his butt off and he kept getting up when he was knocked down. He earned the uniform. He was Acadia's Rudy Ruettiger and he was our hero.

The road to Acadia wasn't lined with comfort and ease for Benji. He worked in the summer, saved his money and applied for a student loan. He knew our family had no financial means to help but that never deterred him.

He packed everything he owned in a big wooden trunk mom had given him, left Georgetown and hitchhiked the 300 kilometres to Wolfville. At Thanksgiving, Christmas and spring break, he would hitchhike back home again. He would often tell us he would be so excited to be home that he would sprint the last quarter mile to the house.

As kids, we would be too busy with the daily goings-on of our own lives to really notice when Benji left. But, we would be shaking like a dog shitting razor blades, waiting from him to return. Those days pre-dated emails and texts, of course. We barely had the means to keep a phone line and, the cost of a long distance call was out of the question.

We never knew the exact date Benji would arrive home but when he finally did, we would go out of our minds – he always brought surprises and was just as happy to see us.

We didn't know it at the time, but Benji was looking out for us. He received a student loan of about $400 for the school year. Of that loan, he would give $200 to our mother so that we could have a few more gifts for Christmas – that is the kind of man my brother Benji is.

A few years later, our youngest sister, Susan, contracted meningitis - she was just four-years-old. For many days it did not look like she was going to survive. She was airlifted to hospital in Halifax where thankfully, she stabilized. Within a few weeks, she was returned to Charlottetown for the long rehabilitation.

My brother Benji hitchhiked from Georgetown to Charlottetown every day to be at her, eat supper with her and to make sure she was never alone. That is the kind of man my brother Benji is.

Like all great men, when you ask him, he downplays the effort. He says the only payback that concerns him is being part of a close family that loves each other and looks out for each other. The standard he has set for all of us remains the creed he lives by. That's the kind of man my brother Benji is.

As the oldest, Benji naturally assumed and thrived in the role of second father after dad passed away in 1996. Throughout the years, he has helped every last one of us with money, assistance, chores and kindness. He has co-signed loans, bought supplies when we needed them, did things for us without taking a penny for his time or asking for anything in return. He and his wife Marie spoil their nieces and nephews with chocolate and toys, and our whole family with love.

And, like he always has, he looks after us still. I can't imagine a life without him.

I love family traditions. I am particularly fond of those that seem unique to our family and those that we carry on even though they have outlived their original necessity. One that fits the bill perfectly for our family is the use of a wall calendar.

I don't mean the use of the wall calendar for its designed purpose. While I imagine paper calendars are becoming less common and will become even more scarce in the future, most homes would still find use for a wall calendar. But, in the King home, the calendar was multi-purposed. It not only showed us the days, dates and special holidays of the year, the back of calendar served as a registry for all things that required jotting down or remembering.

To this day, though new technologies have made it easier to record information, most of my brothers and sisters still use the back of a calendar in similar fashion.

Foolishness on the calendar

Growing up, we played a lot of little games among ourselves for entertainment. We didn't have cable television. We had two channels, CBC on Channel 13 and ATV on Channel 9. Channel 9 was unpredictable and often times the signal was snowy, but back then there wasn't much worth watching on that channel other than the Dukes of Hazzard and The Littlest Hobo. So, our television consumption was limited and we were forced to use our imaginations for fulfillment.

Much of that fulfillment came through competition. Regardless the sport or activity, it was important to win or at least try to outdo one another. There was notoriety in being the fastest runner or for getting the best grades in school, but being the recognized "house prophesier" was the Holy Grail. That moniker brought with it the stature normally reserved for a Stanley Cup champion or a winner of the Georgetown Tug-of-War title.

We never made predictions. My father would ask us to "prophesize" the outcome of events. I loved that word. It seemed rather sophisticated, particularly since my father didn't have much formal education.

When someone in the family was pregnant, my father would instruct my mother to get the calendar off the wall and record everyone's prophecy as to the sex and weight of the child. This wouldn't be limited to just family. It would be extended to all visitors to the King home. The closest to the weight and sex without going over (we used *The Price is Right* rules) was declared the winner.

For as long as I can remember, every calendar in our home would look the same. The face was essentially untouched. But written on the back, in various colors of pen or pencil, were such pertinent prophecies as: the date of arrival of the new calf; the winner of the Eastern Kings Hockey League playoffs; the date of the first snowfall; the winner of the Stanley Cup; or who might be the Georgetown Citizen of the Year.

As you can imagine, the back of our calendar was chalk full of the essential nonsense that fueled life in Georgetown.

Of course, as important as all of those events were, they paled in comparison to politics. Election years trumped all. We needed the big calendars you used to get at the feed mill for election years. They always had the most participants and the person crowned "house prophesier" during election time was God.

The Kings were notorious Liberals - my father Lionel and uncle Jack being poll chairmen for the riding of Kings 5th for many, many years. If the devil himself ran for the Liberals, they would find a way to support him. And, if Jesus himself ran for the Tories, they would find a way to justify not supporting him. Nothing could change their minds.

Many of the visitors to our home were of the same political persuasion, but not all. It led to many spirited discussions around the kitchen table and strained the limits of even the closest friendships.

The PEI provincial election of September 1982 was in full swing. The Tories were running for re-election under the leadership of Premier Jim Lee. The Liberals were trying to get back in power under an impressive but unproven leader in Joe Ghiz. The result was anything but a done deal.

One evening, as the tea brewed in the King home, my father instructed my mother to get the calendar off the wall to record the election winners. My mother managed all the recording on the calendar, but not before my father would give a nod of approval. While Mom was the manager of the calendar, Dad was its CEO.

This particular evening, the table was surrounded and the overflow crowd was forced to find a seat on the cupboard counter or on the floor. As we went around the room, each person would offer his or her thoughts. My mother would ready the pen and look toward my father, who would nod, which meant the information could be dutifully recorded.

The crowd was unanimously in favor of the Liberals. Mike Steele went with 19-13 for the Liberals. My father was more confident, choosing 20-12. And so it continued, 17-15, 24-8 and every other plausible combination to divide 32 seats for the

Liberals in a two-party system. This news was greatly pleasing my father and he was, by all accounts, the full of his shirt.

It went around the table until it was Mickey Clory's turn. Mickey was one of my father's best friends. They would do anything for each other. But, he was also known around house to be a, "Dirty Tory." There were no other kinds of Tories in my father's system of political classification. The Liberal was at the top of the food chain and Dirty Tories were bottom feeders. The only things beneath a Dirty Tory were those who had no known political affiliation. Of those people my father would say, "they claim they are Liberals, but you can't trust the bastards." They were pond scum.

Mickey was well aware his prophesy wasn't going to be met with positive acclaim, but he was asked for his opinion and felt obliged to give it. He cleared his throat and proclaimed that while it may not seem so, he was putting his head before his heart.

"I've been watching it pretty closely Lionel, and I think Jim Lee and the Tories are going to take it 22-10."

The room fell silent. My father didn't look at Mickey. He looked through him. After an awkward silence, Mickey cleared his throat again, took a long sip of his tea and repeated his claim.

"I think Jim Lee and Tories are going to take it 22-10."

The statement was met with the same deafening silence.

My mother stared up at the ceiling, then looked down at the calendar. She had readied the pen to record the contribution, but not surprisingly, the nod of approval never came.

My father threw up his hands, then struck the table with his left fist.

"There is no God-damned way we are going to write a bunch of foolishness on the back of that calendar."

(Note: Jim Lee and PC Party would win the provincial election of 1982 with 22 seats. The Liberal Party won 10 seats. Mickey Clory's prophecy never made the back of the calendar!)

Every April, the wildly popular Burger Love promotion overwhelms Prince Edward Island. The contest sees restaurants create their own speciality burger with locally grown beef. Each burger creation is given a unique name and its contents are introduced to customers like contestants in a championship boxing match. Restaurants vie for the most votes to become Burger Love champion and customers turn out in droves. It has

*become one of the busiest months of the year for local restaurants - a boon
during the non-tourism season.*

The Cattie King Royalty Burger

My mother is a great baker. Her homemade bread and rolls
are legendary. I have never tasted any better and growing up, we
inhaled it by the loaves, with inch-thick butter on top.

Mom was only a fair cook beyond that. Now, to be fair, she
had eight kids to feed daily, so it wasn't as if she had the time or
money to prepare gourmet meals. While she did make a great
boiled dinner, most of her cooking took place on a wood stove
where heat was hard to regulate. She famously overcooked her
food.

I joked once about registering the "Cattie King Royalty
Burger" for the Burger Love competition. It would look something
like this:

*Two, 4oz. Larsen's steak-ette patties, fried at extreme
maximum heat in blackened butter. One side burned nearly
to a crisp, the other side only partially warmed.

*A raw onion sliced so thick a crocodile couldn't fit it all in its mouth.

*One-third slice of no-name cheese, hardened on the corners because it wasn't wrapped properly before being refrigerated.

*Topped with the remnants of runny, no-name ketchup that had to be "rescued" from the bottle by adding a splash of water and shaking it viciously.

*Delicately placed between two heels of week-old Butternut bread.

*Accompanied by a tall glass of ADL Triple Milk or no-name Tang.

I think it might be a Burger Love champion!

I used to write a weekly column for The Eastern Graphic called "The Male Box." It was a young man's view on the world in the early 1990s and often I would share some of the more interesting parts of my childhood. As I was searching for photos at my mother's place, I came across a yellowed copy of this column in her collection. It still makes me smile.

I hadn't thought about that column for many years, but it is funny how time changes a person's perspective. My brother Mark is someone I speak with everyday. He is as much my best friend as he is my brother. I no longer believe I spent my childhood living in his shadow. Today it feels more like I lived beneath his outstretched wings.

We've got Mark. You guys take Denny

I hated him, but I quietly admired him in many ways.

Yes, I laughed when he failed, but I also cheered louder than everyone when he succeeded - which was often.

I forever longed to be better than him, but very early on I accepted the fact it was never going to happen. For a short guy, he cast a long shadow and I hated living in it.

He was my older brother Mark and I kind of hated him. All the little brothers out there will understand.

See, my brother Mark was Wayne Gretzky, Joe Montana, Reggie Jackson and Pele rolled into one. Whether it was a pick up hockey game at Lisa's Pond, a tournament of basement hockey at Flossie's, a football game in Francis Hebert's back yard or a tennis ball baseball game at the old softball field, my brother dominated.

Me, not so much. I was the short, fat, slow goalie who couldn't control rebounds; the short, fat, slow first baseman who always was told to bunt; the short, fat, slow wide receiver with a squeaky voice who was never thrown a pass.

Dad worked until 4:30 p.m. We lived about four miles outside of Georgetown, so my brother and I often arrived late for after-school sporting events. No matter the season, no matter the sport, our late arrival would always be the same.

Our heads would barely be dots on the horizon when someone would notice, stop stick handling and roar loudly, "WE GOT MARK."

The argument would ensue. "No, we got Mark, you guys had first pick." A couple of the older kids would almost go to the knuckles to determine who "got Mark."

Me, not so much.

"You will have to wait for another player to make an even number," I would be told. Or even worse, the other team would pull off a multi-player trade for Mark and often I would be thrown in as part of the trade. I was the infamous, "player to be named later" in most Georgetown after-school sports trades that involved my brother Mark.

Football season was worse. Sure, I was younger and slower than the rest, but I had pretty reliable hands. I fancied myself a perfect short yardage receiver. But, I was the only one who thought that.

Childhood playgrounds can be cruel and discriminating. Such was the case in Georgetown. Two captains would be chosen and the selections would start. Mark would be picked first - every time. The rest of the players would be selected until all that were left were me and my friend Sharon, a tomboy. Sharon would always be chosen before me and before someone could make the final selection, it would be determined that, "you guys take Denny."

My game of football would be to run up the field, then run back. I would move the jackets used to mark the line of scrimmage and the first down line. If things were really going my way, I would get to hike the ball to the quarterback. It was kind of a torturous existence.

Mark would catch four or five touchdowns each game. If that weren't enough, he would also be the rule maker and the game's arbiter if controversy arose. Someone would ask, "That's a touchdown, isn't it Mark?" Or, "Did he go out of bounds Mark?"

I was more studious of the rules of the games than Mark, but it mattered not. Many times, I would have a much better vantage point for the controversial play, but it mattered not. This frustrated me greatly, often to the point where I would pick a fight with my older brother. He'd just push me and laugh, and even more mad. I'd be cursing him, throwing haymakers in his direction until he would knock me down, sit on me and smile.

I'd start to cry and eventually he would let me up. I would scurry away to the school front step like a beaten dog and lick my wounds.

As we got older, I got a bigger and better. Never as good as Mark, but good enough to hold my own. I had a couple of minutes in the spotlight even. I threw a tennis-ball baseball no-hitter and I knocked John Hebert's arm askew as he was getting ready to throw the winning touchdown to Mark. Life has a funny way of working itself out. Regrets?

Yes, I have a few. But, I wouldn't trade any of it for the world.

Memories of Christmas at the King Homestead are my favorite. Everyone always seemed to be in good spirits and there were extra people stopping by the house to visit and spread Christmas cheer. And, of course, we got presents.

Hungry Hungry Hippos

Every Christmas, our Aunt Frances would give us knitted mittens and hats for Christmas. I am certain she did this for all of her dozens of nieces and nephews. The combinations were matching, always two-colored but she was always careful to ensure two kids in the same family received the complimentary patterns. If my hat and mittens were brown with yellow stripes, then it was a good bet that my brother Mark get yellow, with brown stripes.

I remember we would often try to guess the colors before opening the packages each year. We always looked forward to the gifts from Aunt Frances. So much so, that it is usually the first thing we talk about when we discuss family Christmas memories.

The second thing that comes up, is the year Santa Claus gave us Hungry Hungry Hippos. I think it was 1980. We came down the stairs about 39 seconds after Santa Claus had left. As would always happen, Mark would lead the charge and Toby, Susie and I followed in his wake.

We arrived in front of the tree and observed. Our gifts from Santa were never labelled, so we allowed Mark to determine which gifts belonged to which kids. There were two pairs of large boxing gloves, which Mark claimed for him and me. There was a collection of dolls, which Mark allotted to Susie and Toby equally. There were some other insignificant gifts strewn about, but on the coffee table was a rectangular box. On the cover of the box, it read, Hungry Hungry Hippos.

We had seen something similar on television commercials leading up to Christmas and it had been very prominent in the Eaton's catalogue, which we'd had been studying daily since it arrived at the house in September. No one had asked Santa for it, yet there it sat.

Mark stood puzzled, until his crafty mind kicked in, and he proclaimed that, while it was most likely for him, perhaps it would be best if we claimed it as a family gift. This seemed to make sense.

It required four players for a full game and after several arguments, each of us felt satisfied with the adopted hippos we could call our own.

The rules were quite simple: spill the marbles in the middle of the game and use your hippo to gobble up as many marbles as possible. The hippo with the most marbles is the winner. I have no doubt the creators of Hungry Hungry Hippos designed the game to provide maximum entertainment and good-natured fun for its players. That's not what happened at our house. The introduction of Hungry Hungry Hippos led to arguments, fisticuffs and, a few times, blood.

Barely 6 a.m. on Christmas morning, the first game began. The uneven surface tilted and caused the marbles to roll out of the middle and a fight broke out. It deteriorated from there. Every time a game would start, it would be followed by yelling and screaming, and then by tears.

The tears would flow, insults hurled, verbal amends eventually made and the game would start all over again. We competed at Hungry Hungry Hippos as if our lives depended on winning.

Four kids, under 12 pounding on hard plastic hippos, trying to gobble up marbles from a hard plastic game board and fighting to the death like Roman gladiators was just a little bit too much for Dad to handle. Christmas mornings did not bring out the best in him anyway. He would be woefully hung over, lamenting the excess of gifts he couldn't afford and he'd have little patience for the excitement and loudness of the kids at play.

Dad stormed down the stairs, grabbed the game of Hippos and said, "how about we put that away for second." He disappeared with the game. After our initial disappointment, we moved on to play with the other toys and went about our day.

In 1996, after Dad had passed away, our family was cleaning out the old house - mom was going to relocate to a senior citizens unit in Georgetown. We cleared out closets and dressers before hitting the attic. Buried under a series of bags and boxes was *Hungry, Hungry Hippos*. It was the first time we had seen it in more than 25 years. It was in mint condition.

Part 4: There is no place like Georgetown!

I am very proud to have grown up in Georgetown. It's an amazing town full of friendly and kind people. It is also chalk full of amazing characters - which is a storyteller's dream!

People from Georgetown, like many small town folk, have a few quirks about us — we tend to take some quiet joy when others find misfortune, and if that misfortune finds close friends or family, the joy is that much more pleasing. This is how I would best describe Georgetown: if you have a health issue and require a benefit concert, we will gladly have one for you, but we are going to need you to die shortly thereafter. Other places celebrate so-called miracles, where someone was on their deathbed but managed to wrestle themselves from the clutches of death to survive. In Georgetown, that kind of outcome just makes for bad feelings and bad friends.

The Day They Shot Reveen

It was a fall day in the mid 1990s. My sister Toby and her new husband Craig had scored tickets to go see the legendary illusionist and hypnotist Reveen, who was doing a show at the Confederation Centre of the Arts in Charlottetown. The newlyweds were pretty excited to go and no doubt made a bit of a fuss through the town when they had secured the tickets.

Now, as often happens in Georgetown, the fact they were making a fuss about the tickets would have caused many to feel resentment. Not that others would have wanted to go, more that they really just didn't want Toby and Craig to go!

The show was scheduled for Sunday evening. On the Friday before, a car pulled up to our house and out jumped our cousin Myrna. Since she married into our family, Myrna had been a regular - almost daily - visitor to the family house, coming for a chat and to share the news of the day.

This day she walked in the front door and my mother said, "Good morning." Myrna had no time for small talk or pleasantries. She went straight to the kitchen table and sat down. Myrna had some news and was anxious to share it.

As my mother sat down, Myrna slammed her fist on the table and exclaimed quite proudly, "Toby won't be going to see Reveen Sunday!"

Mom tried to explain that Toby had gone into Charlottetown the day before and picked up the tickets. In fact, she told Myrna, Toby was sitting in the very same chair not 12 hours ago and she had seen the tickets with her own eyes.

Undeterred, Myrna proudly exclaimed again, "Nope. Toby won't be seeing Reveen on Sunday…THEY SHOT HIM! It's all over the radio. He's as dead as a nit."

My mother was horrified.

"THEY SHOT HIM? REVEEN? The dear little fellow."

Now, Raveen could have been 6'6" and weighed 300 pounds, it didn't matter. When tragedy struck a victim, my mother would proclaim him to be a, "dear little fellow."

Myrna was making no effort to hide her broad smile at this point.

"Yes, they shot him. And I tell you what, with the show on Sunday there is no way Toby will get her money back for those tickets."

As bad as my mother felt for dear little Reveen, she did not want to see her daughter stuck for tickets. She told Myrna that there was no way the Confederation Centre could charge people for a show that wasn't going to happen. Myrna disagreed however and this greatly perplexed my mother.

After playing some options over in her head, my mother figured the best thing she could do was summon my father into the house. Dad would be puttering around the barn and no doubt having a little "taste" in the process to help him through the day. My mother opened the door and called Dad into the house.

My father would spend most of the day out of the house. In fact, he would normally only be called inside for dinner or supper, or some kind of family emergency. Mom seemed to think this fit the latter.

Dad came in and said hi to Myrna, who went right back into her spiel with a big, broad smile.

"Toby won't be going to see Reveen on Sunday. THEY SHOT HIM! It's all over the radio. He's as dead as a nit."

My father was horrified.

"They shot him? Reveen? The dear little fellow."

Myrna confirmed the news and added a kicker.

"And she won't be getting her money back for the tickets."

Like my mother, dad couldn't see much logic or legality in the Confederation Centre charging for a show that wasn't going to happen. This too perplexed him greatly. After playing over a number of scenarios in his head, my father decided there was only one thing to do – call the Confederation Centre and get to the bottom of it.

My father was born in Boughton Island in 1929. He died in Georgetown in 1996. In that time span, he may have touched the telephone five times. But, this case needed to be dealt with immediately, so he instructed my mother to get out the phone book and call the Confederation Centre.

The phone rang and a pleasant young lady on the other end answered, "Good Afternoon, Confederation Centre of the Arts, how may I help you today?"

My mother promptly said, "Just one second, Lionel wants to talk to you." She handed the phone to dad.

Dad enquired about the refund policy for the Reveen show, stating it would set a terrible precedent to charge for a show that wasn't going to happen. The young lady on the other end of the phone was being very courteous, in spite of the fact she had absolutely no idea what Dad was talking about. She finally asked why he thought the Reveen show would not be happening Sunday.

"THEY SHOT HIM! It's all over the radio. He's as dead as nit," Dad said.

The young lady, as you can imagine, was floored.

"THEY SHOT HIM? REVEEN?"

"Yes," my father replied, "the dear little fellow."

It was getting into the late afternoon on a Friday. The young lady was imagining the influx of calls that were going to come into the box office once the news spreads far and wide. She was in full shock and panic mode. After collecting herself, she used her professional tone to reassure my father that she would do her very best to get to the bottom of the dilemma.

"Mr. King, if you leave me your number I will talk to my supervisor and get back to you when I have a solution."

My father thought this was most impressive. He thanked the young lady and hung the phone up, feeling very pleased with himself for acting quickly. He put his hands behind his head and leaned back in the chair.

"Cattie, could you put the teapot on?"

Mom walked over to the stove to turn the kettle on. As she did, she instinctively turned up the radio that was always on in the kitchen, just as the CFCY news was coming on.

The news jingle finished and newscaster Jimbo Cross began:

"Terrible tragedy in the Middle East today...Israeli president Yitzhak Rabin has been gunned down. He was pronounced dead at the scene."

A big smile came over Myrna's face.

"See Lionel, I told ya. He's dead as a nit!"

We were never much for church.

Our parents gave us a fairly liberal, "take it or leave it" latitude with church. As kids, we took full advantage of the "leave it" part.

We were baptized as Anglicans. Most of the friends I grew up with were Roman Catholic. Even from a very young age, I realized that particular religion seemed to carry with it a great deal of time, work and guilt.

One day I saw one of my friends standing beside the main street in Georgetown. He had a handful of gravel and as a car would happen by, he would throw one of the stones at it. Being Georgetown, he couldn't have been accused of throwing at too many cars. I walked up to him and asked him what the heck he was doing.

"I have to go to confession tomorrow and I want to have something to tell the priest," he said.

It seemed like my Catholic friends were forever going to mass, or confession, or catechism. They were always in church - none of them very happy about it either.

Look Dad...It's a Pirate!

The odd time we would end up in church as children proved very confusing. Because we didn't go to church often, we never really understood the principles of what was going on. We knew Jesus seemed to be a pretty key lad. We could voice along with the Lord's Prayer and we were astute enough to know that when the minister stopped speaking, it was pretty safe to shoot an "Amen."

In fact, one Easter the younger kids in our family went to the Sunday service and upon our arrival back home, Mom asked us how it all went. My sister Toby answered quickly.

"Mom, I think the minister is losing his marbles. We were there for over an hour and he never mentioned the Easter Bunny once."

There were a number of events throughout the year that were connected to the church. Things like church picnics, church suppers, church camps and various other festive events that included food, fun and games. We would want to participate in the good stuff, so we would make our way to church just enough so that we wouldn't stick out during the festivities.

All of that changed, however, when Canon Robert C. Tuck became the minister at Holy Trinity Anglican Church in Georgetown. I suppose when he arrived at the parish, he saw the congregation was smaller than he felt it should have been. I think he took it personally and he dedicated himself to growing the crowd at Sunday service with youngsters like me, regardless of whether we wanted to go or not.

Canon Tuck would best be described as a most ardent and dedicated shepherd to a scattered and reluctant flock. He had the resilience and perseverance of a door-to-door vacuum sales man. You couldn't tell him no. Well, you could tell him no, and I did a million times, but he just wouldn't take no for an answer.

Canon Tuck came from Charlottetown every Sunday. He would stop at our house, come right in the door without knocking and shout, "It's time for church, King Family." It was almost like he was singing. Though it took much prodding and prompting, when he arrived at the parish for service, the youngest of the King family would be in tow. We never made it easy though.

I remember one morning my brother Mark, my sisters Toby and Susie, and I were sitting on the couch watching cartoons on television. We were all decked out in our Sunday best because we knew Tuck would be arriving soon. We heard the car and in unison, we all pretended to be sleeping.

Canon Tuck walked in and sang, "It's time for church, King family." Nobody moved. Not a peep. I fake snored a little. Canon Tuck sang out again, "It's time for church, King family." Still nothing. He came right into the room and grabbed on to me and shook me like he was clearing the screen of an Etch a Sketch. For my sisters and I, the jig was up. We got up and dragged our sorry arses to the car for church.

Mark, however, didn't move. It was as if he was in a coma. Or dead. He stayed like that for minutes. He only came too when Canon Tuck offered to administer mouth-to-mouth resuscitation. Off we went to church.

Quite often in his sermons, Canon Tuck would rail on at length about the ills of society. He seemed to determine that it was all the result of too many people becoming "C and E" Christians. A "C and E" Christian only went to church on the big days of the year: Christmas and Easter.

Every Sunday, I would sit in that fifth pew and I would pray to God to be a "C and E" Christian. If it wasn't for Canon Tuck, I think God would have answered my prayer.

We managed to stay in church long enough to get through confirmation and to partake in communion. To this day, that first offering of the bread and wine was the most disgusting and vile thing I have ever tasted. I was always skeptical about Jesus turning water into wine at the Last Supper but I knew it must have been true because I witnessed Canon Tuck turn wine into cat piss every Sunday at Holy Trinity.

I grew older and God finally answered my prayers. I became a prominent "C and E" Christian. It became easy in

Georgetown, as the flock thinned out after Canon Tuck retired and the church fell into such a state of disrepair that it was only safe to hold service at Christmas and Easter. It suited me great.

One Christmas Eve, our oldest son Jake was three. The new minister was Reverend Montgomery, a tall and lean man with a chiseled chin. He had been the chaplain at Holland College and was a veteran of the Second World War. In fact, he had lost an eye in the war and wore a black patch to cover it, just like the one John Wayne wore in True Grit.

Our family always gathers on Christmas Eve and we try to get to church. This particular year, I was living in Summerside. We were to meet the rest of the family at the church for the service that started at 6 p.m. We arrived promptly at 6:20 p.m.

Now, when you are a "C and E" Christian, there is nothing worse than coming late to one of the two services you will be attending that year. The entire congregation will turn in unison and watch you enter. It's like a walk of shame to the family pew. Now, they say God always waits until the end to judge people, but the congregation at Holy Trinity in Georgetown did not offer the same latitude.

The parking lot was overflowing, indicating a full house had gathered. We could hear they were into one of the hymns as we made our way into the foyer. We quietly kicked the snow off our boots and we waited in the foyer behind the big doors until the congregation finished a beautiful version of *Joy to the World*.

When the organ stopped, I opened the door as lightly as I could. It creaked just a little but nobody turned around. We seemed to be home free. We started for the family pew as Reverend Montgomery turned around. He had the Bible in his left hand. As he lifted his arms to lead the next prayer, he picked up his head and focused his one-eyed gaze upon us.

Little Jake stopped. He gasped. His eyes opened widely and he roared at the top of his lungs, as only a three-year old child in shock can roar.

"LOOK DAD, IT'S A PIRATE!"

We made that long walk of shame to the King family pew.

When Canon Robert Tuck
came to Georgetown, he
dragged the King family to
church every Sunday.

Two larger than life characters and
gentlemen from Eastern PEI – MP
Lawrence MacAulay presenting
Georgetown Citizen of the Year Award to
Clarence MacSwain.

A rare occasion when Georgetown Mayor Charlie Martell was captured
wearing a suit. He was a blue-collar mayor for a blue-collar town.

(Above) Overlooking Boughton Island, the majestic and mythical birthplace of the King family. *(Below)* Though the Kings left Boughton Island in the 1940s, family members maintained a deep love and connection to their birthplace. The connection remains strong to this day with the King children and grandchildren. Most of us most make an annual trek to "the Isle" to walk in the footsteps of our ancestors.

My uncle Donald King offering sage advice at my wedding reception in Summerside. Of all the storytellers I have ever known, he was the best.

Howard "Binx" MacLean (pictured with his lovely wife Eleanor after he being named Georgetown Citizen of the Year in the early 1980s. Binx was a community leader and builder, as well as a key figure in many classic Georgetown stories.

My brother Lloyd (far right, front) photographed with his work pals at the local fish plant. Lloyd has always had a terrific ear for a good story, along with a God-given ability to make people laugh. His stories are simply hilarious. A true mark of a great story is that you never grow tired of hearing it. Lloyd's fish plant stories never miss the mark.

Our first family portrait from our brother Benji's wedding in Moncton, NB in 1980. It was also our first family trip off PEI. Back (from left) Peggy, Pammy, Cattie (Mom), Lionel (Dad), Marie, Benji, Lloyd. In the front, Susie, Toby, Mark and me. Apparently, I was positioned in the photo to hide Lloyd's mismatched dress pants!

October 3, 1959. My parents Lionel and Cattie were married. Standing for them were Joe and Martha Kinnear (Martha was Dad's sister). I have often heard they spent their honeymoon digging potatoes at Rupert Wight's farm in Burnt Point. I don't know if it is true, but it makes a heck of a good story!

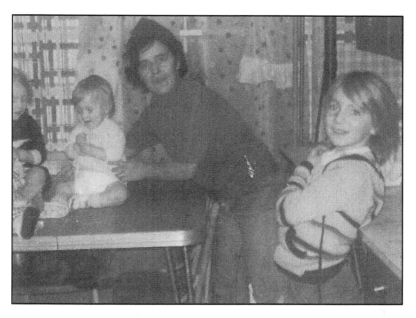

A regular day at the King Homestead! Mom was the busiest person I have ever met. Though often overwhelmed with life and reality, she always loving and caring. Here she is keeping an eye on Toby (left) and baby Susie, while Pammy looks on. Our family was always closely knit, and though we argue and disagree by times, we remain very close.

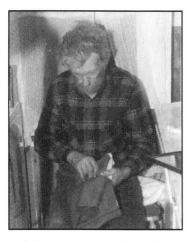

Christmas morning at the King homestead. Lionel, wearing his trademark work shirt and pants, opening up a gift. Judging by the hair and demeanor, he looks to be suffering from a Christmas Eve hangover!

My brother Mark after a game of hockey (with Dad's old Ford half-ton in the driveway). Whatever team Mark played on, he always led the team (and often the league) in scoring. I am proud of his accomplishments now, but growing up in his shadow was difficult and frustrating for me!

Frank MacDonald owned Cottage Farm in Georgetown Royalty. He talked in a loud, rural Island voice and addressed everyone he met as "Doc." I visited the farm often with my father and learned quickly that Frank was a true Georgetown character!

(Left) John "Eloi" Doiron enjoying a drink and a chat with my brother Lloyd at the annual seniors Christmas social hosted by the local Lions Club. Eloi worked at the Georgetown Shipyard with my father and during break times, would tell many stories. Most were tall tales that were hard to believe and always portrayed Eloi as the hero. The stories entertained my father greatly and he appreciated Eloi's storytelling gifts.

"The Cowboy" Mike Steele was my father's best friend. I enjoyed a lifetime of great adventures with those two.

Walter Boudreault was a mechanical genius and a unique character. He was double-jointed and would often contort his body to fit inside a small oven.

Two of Georgetown's funniest people Hibbie Jenkins (left) and Teddy Easton (wearing a clothespin on his nose!) Teddy's role as "Georgetown Santa" has become legendary in my hometown.

The Christmas tree at the King homestead was not something you would find on a Hallmark greeting card!

Lionel would sit for hours in a chair and knit heads (twined-mesh used in lobster traps).

This photo accurately reflects the chaos of Christmas morning at the King homestead in the early 1980s. Peggy is on the right, looking through a Fisher-Price View Finder, while Mom and Dad appear to be trying to figure out how to open a box of Lego. Undoubtedly, Dad would have been much more interested in drinking his tea. Regardless of the time of day, or what the occasion, I can hardly remember my father sitting at the kitchen table without a cup a tea in front of him.

One time I dressed up as Georgetown Santa — and did not fool any of the kids in the local kindergarten class.

The four youngest Kings (Me, Mark, Susie and Toby) engaged in a "fight to the death" game of Snakes and Ladders. The coffee table in the living room was unstable, therefore we had to place the game on the floor to literally level the playing field. We always found ways to entertain ourselves.

We moved to the King Homestead in 1973. Some of my most memorable days were spent there and that home still means the world to me. My brother Benji and I bought the house in 1998 and we still use it as a summer residence. We continue to make family memories there which would make my father very proud.

Flossie MacConnell (second from right) was my mother's sister and was like a second mother to us. When we weren't at home, we were at Flossie's and most likely were up to no good! Pictured (from left) are Barb Mazerolle (nee MacConnell), Mrs. Eileen MacConnell and the bride, Bunny.

During Georgetown Summer Days, Mike Steele was asked to dress up as The Town Crier. Steele was always a great sport and never said "no" to anyone.

106

This photo was taken at the foot of Glenelg Street in Georgetown. At left is the historic Georgetown Jail and Courthouse. At right, is the Baptist church and in back is the old Georgetown Rink.

My father always wanted to be a farmer and was forever trying to make an extra buck raising livestock. Here he is feeding some cattle, with the help of grandchildren Brad and Melinda. One of these animals may be the famed "Hateful Bull!"

Marty Dalton grew up next door to my mother. Like most fortunate to call Georgetown home, Marty is a unique character who enjoys a good story and a good laugh.

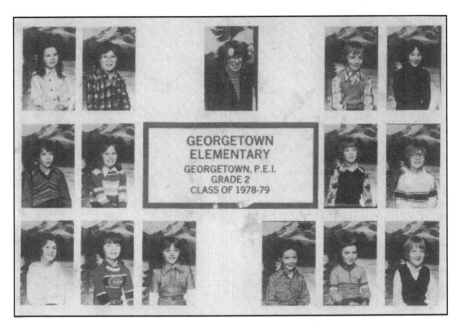

My grade two class photo (I am second from the right on the bottom row). My bangs would indicate that my early haircuts were of the homemade variety! My classmates: (top)Barb Martell, Shane Martell, Mrs. Miriam Smith, Mark Campbell, Benita MacConnell. (middle) Daryl Batchilder, Bobbi-Jo MacLean, Sharon Hebert, Shane Brousseau. (bottom) Jaynie MacKenzie, Carter Gotell, Melina Sheppard, Shane Yorston, me and Pat Murphy.

Waldron Lavers(right) was a fixture in many of my Dad's stories. In the election of 1978 he ran as a Liberal candidate with running-mate Arthur MacDonald and Premier Alex Campbell. Arthur and Premier Campbell won election, but Waldron fell short, losing to Lowell Johnston.

The other side of our family, the Stevens, are also characters. Here they are gathered for some type of family occasion at aunt Maizie's place. My mom is second from the right, and my father is in the very front with his back to the camera. We are unsure of the occasion, but it appears to have been a cold day!

The building that housed the old pool hall in Georgetown. It was one of our favorite hangouts. Many of us cried when they tore that building down!

It was a monumental challenge, and it provided the basis for my father's most famous story, but eventually the townsfolk worked together to build the Georgetown Rink. I don't remember the building, but its legend is burned into my heart.

My aunts Flossie (left) and Maizie, two of my mother's sisters. They were funny, devilish and enjoyed a good time. They were giants in my life.

Mark thinks this his him. I think it is me. It's a 35-year debate. Santa left goalie gear one Christmas with no nametag attached. We both claimed the prized gift.

Mike Steele's last birthday celebration. Liked by all who knew him, he is an "awful miss."

Bernard Keenan was a great friend to my father and a regular visitor to the King homestead.

Francis Hebert built road hockey nets for us and drove me to every minor hockey game I ever played. He was a great man.

My uncle Jack King, a charter member of the Boughton Island Poets Society, and a master storyteller.

Three Georgetown legends (from left) Bernard Batchilder, Ray Lavandier and Albert King. Ray operated The Lucky Dollar corner store and was famous in the town for many endeavors, like organizing local boxing matches and roller-skating disco parties at the rink. Like all legends, they live on long after they are gone.

Long-time Member of Parliament Hon. Lawrence MacAulay (left) surprised The Four Tellers during the final show of the 2015 season. It was a crowning moment of the season. David Weale, Gary Evans, Alan Buchanan and I were delighted with the appearance.

Jimmy MacConnell was a great supporter of the Georgetown community, even after his death. At his wake, visitors were asked to throw cash into his casket. Over $1500 was donated to the rink.

As part of The Four Tellers, I get the chance to share the great stories and characters of my hometown on the stage of the Kings Playhouse in Georgetown. It is an honor and a privilege.

Often times you hear a story for the first time and it may not resonate with you right away. It may take hearing it a few times to gain a full appreciation. But, there are also stories you hear that immediately strike a chord with you. The story of Roy and Mae fit the latter category for me and my friends in Georgetown.

This is also one of the very first stories I remember being widely told and enjoyed broadly. This was a story that became legendary and an instant classic in my hometown. If you lived in Georgetown in the mid 1980s you would have heard and told this story hundreds of times. And, though almost 30 years has passed since I first heard it, it remains well-known, well-told and much-appreciated.

Roy and Mae

Roy and Mae were an older couple in Georgetown. They were not married in the eyes of the law. They were "shacked up."

They were opposite of each other in almost every way. Mae was thin and rather tall for a woman. Though kind at heart, she was mostly stern, serious and did not appear to enjoy life much. Roy was more outgoing. He was short with a big, round belly. In fact, if you looked at him from the shoulders down, the shape of

115

his remaining body would look like the number nine. Roy was also known to be fond of the drink.

It was often said, in Georgetown circles, that Mae did not like Roy when he was drinking and Roy could not stand Mae when he was sober. In spite of this challenge, they somehow made it work and stayed together for a number of years.

Prince Edward Island was one of the last provinces in Canada to adopt legislation making it mandatory to wear seatbelts while operating a vehicle. Our sister province Nova Scotia had beaten us to it, but only by a year or so.

Roy and Mae decided to make a road trip to Nova Scotia to visit family. It was a lovely summer afternoon. They took the ferry boat from Wood Islands, PEI to Caribou, NS and after disembarking, Roy and Mae headed for Pictou.

They had been in the car for barely a few moments when Roy noticed the red and blue lights of an RCMP cruiser behind him. Roy signalled and pulled over. As the officer was heading toward the car, Roy grabbed the seat belt and swung it over his arm.

The RCMP officer leaned on the car, looked inside and informed Roy he had been pulled over because he was not wearing his seat belt, which was a violation of the highway traffic act.

Roy looked into the eyes of the officer and rather defiantly replied, "I was certainly wearing my seatbelt."

It was not the response the officer had expected. In fact, he was caught off guard by Roy's terse reply. Keeping his professional tone and demeanor, he again explained why he pulled the vehicle over.

"I was following behind you and it was quite evident you were not wearing your seatbelt therefore I am legally obligated to give you a ticket."

Roy, a bit more agitated, was steadfast in his view.

"To hell with your ticket. I was wearing my seatbelt," Roy said.

The RCMP officer was flabbergasted. As hard as he tried to convince Roy of the seat belt violation, Roy was hearing none of it and remained defiant.

"You weren't wearing your seat belt, I could clearly see," the officer said.

"You saw wrong," Roy replied. "I had it on the whole time."

The stalemate continued. The officer noticed Mae in the passenger seat. She hadn't said a word the whole time. In fact, she seemed to be paying no attention whatsoever to the discussion. Mae was staring out the passenger window.

As a final plea, the officer leaned into the car and addressed Mae.

"Ma'am, you are the only witness to this violation. It is quite obvious to me that this gentleman wasn't wearing a seat belt. For whatever reason he won't admit to it. We have been arguing back and forth here for 10 minutes so I am going to have to ask for your thoughts."

After a few seconds, Mae turned around and looked directly at the officer and said, "Officer I don't know why you would even bother. There's no use trying to talk any sense into that man when he's drunk!"

My brother Lloyd is a brilliant storyteller. No matter how big or small the room, Lloyd is usually the funniest person in it and the centre of attention. He also has a razor sharp memory for stories from before I was even born. I love when he shares a new gem with me, as he did with this one in the summer of 2015.

Dr. Aitken comes to Georgetown

Every June for many years, Dr. Melville Aitken and his wife would leave Toronto and come to their Georgetown summer home on Water Street. I only knew Dr. Aitken when he was an old man, as my father used to do odd yard jobs for him. Dad would limb trees, clean around flowerbeds, pick up his garbage and do any other jobs required.

One day, my brother Lloyd and his friend Eric Jenkins were asked to do some raking for the Aikens in their garden. Upon completion, their cash payments were presented in white envelopes inscribed with the message, "To the boys who did the rakin' for Mrs. Aitken."

During his first visit to Georgetown, in the late 1960s, Dr. Aitken left his summer home and walked down Water Street toward the Queen's Wharf. It was obvious he was very pleased with his choice of summer residence and he wanted to drink in all its splendor on what was a gorgeous morning.

Dr. Aitken walked down along the wharf, watched the lobster fishing boats return from their morning haul and he was enjoying life that was so far removed from the daily grind of Toronto.

After chatting with a few fishermen and making small talk with some of the locals, Dr. Aitken turned to head back up Water Street. As he strolled, he saw his property from a new perspective and was impressed with the rugged cliff and red shoreline.

Rather than walk up the paved road, he ventured over toward the shore. The tide was low which allowed the good doctor to stroll along and admire the shallow pools of water that had formed. He put his hands on his hips and squinted his eyes as he stared toward the Island sun. He was truly in a blissful place. Just then, he noticed a large blue heron soaring in the sky.

Dr. Aitken had never seen such a creature and he watched, almost spellbound, as the heron seemingly floated, its wings spread wide, searching the shallow water pools for a morning snack. The majestic creature soared for about five minutes and Dr. Aitken enjoyed every single second. Just as the heron landed on the beach, a young Georgetown resident happened by.

Lawrence was just strolling the beach to pass the time, as he often did. Lawrence was a typical Georgetown kid - friendly but not cultured in the ways of the world beyond the town borders. Lawrence, who talked with a slow, rural Island drawl, said good morning to Dr. Aitken and then quickly asked what the visitor was doing on the beach.

Dr. Aitken explained he was overwhelmed by the sight and completely captivated by the incredible flying creature he had just witnessed. He was also at a loss to explain what exactly he had been admiring. In all his years on the earth, Dr. Aitken told Lawrence, he had never seen such a sight.

"My dear boy, what do the good people of Georgetown call such a beautiful creature?"

Lawrence did not want to disappoint his new friend.

"Well sir, I don't know what you lads up there in Toronto call them, but down here in Georgetown we just call them biiiiiiirrrddds."

I am from one of the last generations of big families. It is a tremendous gift.

There are eight kids in our family. The McConnells, our cousins, had 13. The Jenkins, who were close friends, had 13 or 14. It seemed everyone came from a large family. Times were different then. And much simpler.

Take Christmas as an example. Today, we take our kids to holiday activities: parades, parties and such. Events are ready-made and pre-packaged. Today's parents almost work too hard to try to create the Christmas magic.

It was far different in Georgetown. Life's lessons were often learned the hard way. Dreams could be shattered with very little remorse or concern for one's emotional state. I'm not saying it was right or wrong, but that was just how it was.

Like the time I found out about Santa Claus. I was nine.

Likely for financial reasons as much as convenience, we would often find ourselves celebrating special occasions like Easter or Thanksgiving with a number of families. But not just the big holidays. I remember every year we would walk in a convoy, sometimes as many as 60 or 70 kids, from Georgetown to the old Brudenell Park to celebrate the Queen's Birthday. We would always have a lunch packed that contained Kraft Sandwich Spread sandwiches, a Joe Louis cake and a Miracle Whip jar filled with Freshie or No-Name Tang. No matter how hard my mother tried to wash it, you could always taste the residue of the miracle whip around the rim of the jar.

But, of all the holidays, there was nothing like Christmas.

Georgetown Santa

Christmas is so different today compared to when I was young. At our house, our kids open one gift at a time and they take the time to read the tags and the cards. They open the presents carefully, as if uncasing a bomb. Everything seems so structured and organized. The whole process takes a couple of hours now.

Christmas morning for us was NOT like that. We would wake up at 5:30 a.m. and as soon as our feet hit the floor, we would be on the dead run. Down stairs we would fly. Seconds later, the gifts under the tree would have evaporated. We didn't care about tags and cards or even who the gifts were for. I walked around one Christmas day until about 2:30 in the afternoon with a box of tampons. I couldn't understand why the string wasn't long enough to tie to my belt buckle. It turns out they weren't for me!

We never went to malls or parades to see Santa Claus. Santa would always come to us, usually a few days before Christmas, usually at our Aunt Flossie's house.

Flossie was one of my mother's sisters. She was like a second mother to us and her house provided the setting for many of our most poignant memories. Flossie's was better than Disney World for us.

This particular Christmas, we had all gathered at Flossie's. About 50 or 60 kids were jammed into the little bungalow and we were bouncing off the walls with anticipation of seeing Santa Claus.

But, Georgetown Santa didn't quite look like the guy on the cover of the Eaton's catalogue.

Georgetown Santa always walked down the road from up where Teddy Easton lived. I always just figured he was giving the reindeer some much needed rest before the big trip. Georgetown Santa wore rubber boots with red soles, exactly like the ones you would buy at Munroe's War Surplus in Montague. While Georgetown Santa wore a lovely red coat with white fur on it, he also wore a pair of green work pants with grease stains.

Georgetown Santa's hands were full of calluses and he had dirt under his fingernails. It was as if the elves had gone on strike and Santa was forced to build all the toys by himself. But, when you are nine years old, it is very easy to suspend belief and to oversee such trivial matters.

This particular Christmas, Georgetown Santa was walking down the road toward Flossie's. We were watching through the picture window. A light dusting of snow was falling - those big, fat snowflakes that seem to always fall on Christmas Eve. The streetlights let off a romantic glow. It was the most beautiful sight my eyes had ever seen, almost like a Norman Rockwell painting, wrapped up in one of those magical snow globes.

Suddenly Georgetown Santa waved at us and we collectively lost our minds.

Georgetown Santa came into the house with a "HO HO HO." His hosts pulled up a chair just off the kitchen table and Georgetown Santa took a seat. A couple of my uncles shook his hand, slapped him on the back and set a tall glass beside him.

Georgetown Santa guzzled it down in one drink. The glass was re-filled. I figured it was water and Ol' St. Nick was dry from his journey down the road. It was water alright, but the Holy kind. Johnny Perry had distilled it earlier in the month.

The house was abuzz. Kids were lining up and butting in front of each other, pushing and ripping and tearing as anxious kids do. Someone got clipped in the mouth which forced one of the older cousins to take charge.

"Ok. We will line three up here in the living room and the rest of you can go in the back bedroom. We will take you out three at a time, oldest to youngest."

This seemed to suit everyone just fine. Except me. I was one of the youngest. I didn't like always being left to the last.

"Stop cryin' and just go along," my cousin shouted at me. Dear God, when I die they should inscribe that on my tombstone. Having no other say in the matter, I went along to the back room.

The wood stove was snapping. It was about 160 degrees Celsius in the kitchen. Old time Christmas carols played on the record player. People were laughing and kids were taking turns sitting on Georgetown Santa's knee, telling him what they wanted for Christmas. Georgetown Santa would roar, "HO! HO! HO!"

When one child would climb down off the knee, Georgetown Santa would have another drink from the glass as the next child arrived. It was a truly wonderful night.

We were about half way through the pile of kids and I hadn't seen Santa yet. I was getting antsy. But, I wasn't crying and I was trying my level best to just go along.

At the same time, the night was starting to catch up with Georgetown Santa. The heat and the holy water were taking their toll. Georgetown Santa was starting to slur his words a little. It wasn't so much a, "HO! HO! HO!" Now, it was more of a gurgled, "Huh – Huh –Huh."

It was almost time for me to make my way to the living room when out in the kitchen there arose such a clatter. One of my drunken uncles screamed, "What in Christ is the matter?"

One of the older kids ran in and said, "Oh my God! Santa's dead!"

We all ran out of the back room. Georgetown Santa wasn't in the kitchen anymore. Nobody was. The front door was open and we ran out onto the step to see what was going on.

It was as if someone took that snow globe and smashed it with a ballpeen hammer.

Georgetown Santa was laying on the road. His beard was gone. His jacket was open. He rolled over onto all fours and was dry-heaving. Four or five of my uncles grabbed him under the arms and began dragging him back up the road from where he came. It was a horrific site. My Aunt Flossie was furious.

I couldn't go along any longer. I started to cry.

I looked at Flossie, big tears in my eyes and said, "Santa's dead, what are we going to do for Christmas now?"

As I had warned, life's lessons were often learned the hard way in Georgetown, with very little concern for the fragility of a young child.

She looked at me and said, "Now you are one fool aren't ya. That's not Santa Claus. That's Teddy Easton. And he's drunk. He's not dead. But if I see the son of a whore tomorrow, he's gonna wish he was dead!"

I learned from my father that the best storytellers are able to walk a fine line. Part of the art is being able to tell stories about others without being overly offensive, and to make sure the story doesn't appear to be mocking.

Many times my dad crossed over the line. I have too. You never really know you've gone too far, until you have gone too far!

I have always found the best way to neutralize such a situation is to be sure to include stories about yourself, so that others have the opportunity to enjoy a good laugh at your expense. I think it's a storyteller's way of sharing in the fun, or begging for forgiveness.

Jack Daniels and the Dry Heaves

One of the first summer jobs I had was working as a general laborer at an indoor trout farm in Georgetown. International Marine Harvesting Ltd. was located in the old seafood processing plant that had been closed due to bankruptcy years earlier. It was one of the biggest indoor trout operations in the world with more than 30 large tanks holding trout that were from an inch long to more than 20 pounds. It was a great concept that failed miserably.

Before its demise, I had scored a summer gig there. It was a 9-5 job and the decent pay cheque provided me with the means for a great "coming of age" summer in Georgetown. And a great summer it was.

I was 16. My friends and I were starting to rebel, as teenagers often do. We would pick away at the beer on weekends. We would hang out in the evenings and devise new ways of trying to get a girlfriend without actually having a conversation with one.

My friend Carter had just a little more gumption than the rest of us. Somehow, he managed to connect with a girl named Lori, who lived in Toronto but was spending part of the summer in Georgetown with her extended family. Lori spoke differently. She wore cooler clothes and, mostly because we hadn't been looking at her every day for 16 years, was prettier than the other girls we knew.

She took a bit of a shine to Carter and they were an item. As we got to spend more time with Lori and the other girls, I started to realize that girls were normal and fun, and some of them even enjoyed my company.

It turned out Lori had a sister, Renee. She was just a bit younger but she was blonde and cute, and seemed to gravitate toward me when we would gather for a bonfire or any other type of after-dark summer activity. This meant nothing to me of course. Had she been wearing a large sign flashing, "I like you," I would have still struggled to figure it out.

This perplexed young Renee. Toronto girls were used to boys being more forward and after a couple of weeks of barely getting much more than a pulse from me, she decided to tell her sister, to tell Carter, to tell me that I should ask out Renee.

So Carter told me and I immediately broke out in a cold sweat. Carter reassured me that I should just be myself, make her laugh and everything would work out. He gave me explicit instructions.

"Don't go putting on a big show or you will wind up just making an arse of yourself."

Pretty sage advice really.

Everything was set in motion. A group of us would gather behind the old pool hall after dark, we would get a few beers, sit around and enjoy the summer evening. Once things settled in, Carter would ensure Renee and I sat together and that we could move the relationship along.

Enter Derek Johnson. Derek has been my best friend since I was two years old. He is a couple of years older than I am but he always saw fit to include me in the "older guys'" activities. He did this because it brought him great entertainment. He once convinced me to try to get into the Cardigan Liquor Store when I was about 15. I got about one foot in the door and the attendant starting chasing me, telling me he would kick my arse all the way to Georgetown if he saw me in there again. Derek just about keeled over laughing. *(FYI - I have always had a baby face and was checked for ID at bars and liquor stores until I was almost 30.)*

Derek got wind of the potential set up and decided he should help get me ready for the occasion. He took Carter and me for a drive in his red Toyota Tercel and began his counsel.

"Let's go to the liquor store and get a bottle of whiskey. It will calm your nerves and help you feel more comfortable," Derek said.

It seemed to make so much sense at the time. Derek would get the booze, drop us off at home to get showered and dressed for the evening, he would then pick us up and we would spend a couple of hours drinking before the girls would arrive.

The scheme was hatched, and smelling of Brut 33, we piled into Derek's car. He began to tell us why whiskey would be better for us, it was smoother and unlike rum, it wouldn't bring out the "pretend fighter" in us. It all seemed to make so much sense.

Derek pulled out a bottle of Jack Daniels. It was a pint, which we have always referred to as a "point." He handed me the bottle and said, "take a drink." Which I did. I took a big drink, and lowered it to almost half. I'd drunk whiskey with Derek before and knew he liked his Jack Daniels straight, so even though my throat and upper lungs were on fire, I didn't bother to ask for any chaser.

We cruised around for a while longer until dark. I was feeling great and for the first time in my life, feeling very confident about my opportunity with Renee. At dark, we pulled in behind the pool hall and got out. A crowd had gathered. Carter went and stood beside Lori and I went directly beside Renee. She smiled at me.

Derek landed back with the whiskey, sneaked it into my hand and said, "Take another drink, it will settle you down." It seemed to make so much sense. So I took another drink. A big one. I finished the bottle.

Renee watched me do this. She seemed impressed. She smiled at me again. We moved closer to each other. I even put my arm around her and she didn't seem to mind. We sat around and told some stories and talked about the stuff that sex-charged teenagers talk about on summer nights.

It all seemed to be going so well. I was entertaining Renee. She was giggling and laughing. I could sense in my heart that I was going to get the chance to make out with her. Then someone turned out the lights. That someone was Jack Daniels.

I remember being laid out flat on the ground, face down in the green grass behind the old pool hall. As I would throw up, Derek would grab my ankles and pull me a few feet backwards. Renee though, was sticking by me, she was rubbing my back and telling me I was going to be ok.

I would throw up some more, Derek would move me and that continued until there was nothing left inside my stomach. I had even run out of bile. I had never been so sick in my life. Renee, though, stuck with me, right by my side.

I began wretching and gagging again. Every time I would gag, nothing would come out of my mouth, but the pressure of the dry heave would cause me to let out a big, loud fart. I repeated it four or five times, each time the fart getting louder and longer.

I think Renee left after the second fart. I don't think I ever saw her again. Derek, like only Derek can do, stood beside me and after each gag and subsequent fart, he would ask me, "Are you sick?"

I couldn't answer. All I remember was thinking, "How did it all go so wrong?"

It seemed to make so much sense at the time.

Part 5: Georgetown Characters

One of the world's great humorists and storytellers, Mark Twain, once wrote, "Truth is stranger than fiction, but it is because fiction is obliged to stick to possibilities; truth isn't."

Twain's comment also applies to characters. Georgetown, like most of small towns in Prince Edward Island, is full of great characters - people so unique that, if they did not exist in real life, it would be impossible to create them.

I have often thought if a great film director, such as a Martin Scorcese, visited Georgetown, he would never leave. To be immersed in so many characters, be they funny or tragic, would no doubt lead to multiple Oscar victories. Not to mention the endless entertainment!

Like me, my father loved to observe the many characters that called Georgetown home. It brought him endless hours of laughter and smiles. I expect he found out at some point what I have recently discovered – part of the magic of the true character is not realizing you are one!

Charlie Martell, the Blue Collar Mayor

Wherever he went, with whomever he talked, the late Charlie Martell left an impression.

Charlie was much older than me. In spite of the age gap, I often viewed us as kindred spirits. In fact, later in life we became quite good friends. Charlie would often drop in to visit when I worked for the provincial government or stop by the house when I lived in Georgetown Royalty. Normally, Charlie had an angle or a project he was working on and that project would be something that would promote or enhance daily life in Georgetown.

Of all of the people I have known, I cannot think of anyone who loved and promoted Georgetown with any more passion than Charlie Martell.

Charlie had strong opinions on social and political issues. Often they collided with mine. He had trouble finding a home with the mainstream political parties, but his personality was best suited being politically untethered. Our chats would often get heated, but we always enjoyed the opportunity to hash out those dicey topics and to depart on friendly terms.

Charlie was a long-serving Mayor of Georgetown and he was perfect for the times. During his tenure, Georgetown was in the latter stages of an industrial boom period, with a large seafood processing facility, a lumber yard, flourishing fisheries and of course, the Georgetown Shipyard. Georgetown was a blue collar town and its mayor was fittingly blue collar to the bone.

Charlie worked at the Shipyard. Often when he was needed for a TV or newspaper interview, the media would find him at his job site and Charlie would skirt off to answer their questions. There were no shirts and ties or any type of wardrobe pageantry. Charlie would walk out in his coveralls, hard helmet and safety glasses and begin the interview. Some of my fondest memories are watching Charlie as he wore a blue hard helmet that had a pair of protective ear muffs on the top -- his scraggly black and grey hair underneath whipping in the wind.

There were no airs about Charlie. He simply represented the town the only way he knew how. And, the townsfolk appreciated him for it.

As I look back, I realize Charlie was an important figure throughout my life. In many ways, though his exterior may not have suggested it, Charlie was equal parts genius, innovator and conspiracy theorist, with a social conscience that would make Maude Barlow and David Suzuki envious.

I often thought Charlie was ahead of his time. Charlie dreamed up the brilliant idea of subdividing housing lots on Victoria Street and offering them for sale to prospective new residents for $1. Still today, that area of the town is referred to as "The Dollar Lots" or "Loonie Lane", even though it is closer to $1500 for a fully serviced lot purchase today. While there have been close to a dozen new homes constructed, almost all were constructed by existing town residents. Though it may not have had the desired impact of increasing the town's population, Charlie's scheme increased the residential tax base.

I think if such an idea were concocted today, with the power and connectivity of social media, there would have been an even larger, more positive result.

When it came to Georgetown, Charlie always dreamed of a big score. He led the charge to rebuild the King's Playhouse after the original building burned down in 1982. He wanted to build a golf course. He wanted the town to diversify, to become more focused on senior-friendly housing and seasonal tourism. Many of those ideas are coming to fruition in Georgetown today, thanks I believe to the seeds Charlie sowed years ago.

What I loved most about Charlie was that he was very much a walking contradiction. While he dreamed of big things for Georgetown and worked tirelessly toward that end, he was also very critical of plans or developments that might change the personality and identity of the town. He was open to many ideas, but his mind would close quickly to others.

Like me and my brothers Mark and Lloyd, Charlie loved to gamble. He played the 6-49 and Super 7 religiously. He scratched and pulled tickets habitually. He cursed Atlantic Lottery Corporation up and down for what he essentially determined was a crusade to ensure he never won anything, yet he had amassed what must have been one of the world's largest and most diverse collections of scratch tickets. He had thousands of them, from Saudi Arabia, to Croatia and from every other country you could imagine.

As he did when he was mayor, in his personal life Charlie always looked for the big score. But, he professed to all who would listen of his desperate poor gambling luck.

We would often sit at Daryl's General Store and read the Pro-Line sports odds sheet like some Wall Street brokers would read the stock market report. Charlie would regale us with stories of times he had spent at the racetracks in Toronto playing the ponies.

"If I would have spent as much time studying at school as I did studying the horse lines at Woodbine, I would have been a lawyer," Charlie would tell us. We would laugh.

Charlie would also tell us about how "jinxed" he was in the field of gambling. One day he told us about the time he had overheard a tip from a veteran handicapper at Woodbine. There was a horse with long 88-1 odds and word was it was going to have a miracle trip and win. Charlie loved a good tip, and he convinced his friend to pool their money and they loaded up the horse with every cent they had. The starting gates opened and the long shot sprung to the front as if it was shot out of a cannon. He continued to open up over the field until he was about 35 lengths ahead turning for the home stretch.

Charlie told us he looked at his friend and said, "They can't catch him now. As long as he doesn't die, we are going to cash in."

As soon as he said it, the horse collapsed, sending the jockey flying through the air. The horse never moved. The rest of the field caught up and went past, leaving Charlie in shock.

The friend was even more disgusted. He threw the tickets on the ground and told Charlie it was time to go home. Charlie could not take his eyes of the horse. He told his friend he was not leaving until the horse got across the finish line. After the vets and stable hands spent considerable time, they realized the horse had breathed its last. Ten or 15 minutes later, a Caterpillar front-end loader scooped up the horse and started backing up toward the finish line.

"As he crossed the finish line, all I could hear was the BEEP, BEEP, BEEP of the loader…that's the kind of luck I have betting!"

We lost Charlie a few years back. I miss him greatly. Every time I hear the BEEP, BEEP, BEEP of a loader, I smile and think of him.

I hope he is somewhere chasing a big score.

Many of the stories my father would tell us were from - or about - the men he worked with at the Georgetown Shipyard.

The Yard, as he called it, was ground zero for characters, comedic artists, practical jokers and storytellers. Some of the events that happened there became folklore in my hometown, like the time Dennis Clory sent the new employee to get two buckets of steam. Half an hour later the newbie returns carrying two five-gallon buckets of boiling water with a piece of plywood covering each bucket. They still laugh about this many years later.

My father would tell us about the goings on at The Yard regularly. There were funny stories. There were tall tales. The ones that would make my father shake his head and laugh at the same time were the ones he would tell us about his co-worker John Doiron.

Quite the Bucko was Eloi Doiron

His given name was John, but for reasons we may never know, he was known as Eloi. He was short and plump. He had thick glasses similar to the ones worn by the cartoon character, Mr. Magoo. He was perhaps best known for operating a small bootlegging operation to supplement his Shipyard income.

As far as I ever knew, which was as much as my father told me, Eloi had never traveled far or done much of historic consequence outside of the borders of Georgetown. In spite of this, Eloi would tell story after story at the Shipyard - each tale portraying himself as the star or the centre of the narrative.

The men knew the stories weren't true, as Eloi likely did himself. But they were entertaining and became legendary as Eloi would try to outdo himself each time. My father thought this was great.

The workers would sit around the lunchroom and Eloi would rattle on. One time, he told them, he went to a dance in back of Montague. He danced all night and drank just short of a 40-ouncer of black rum. When the dance ended, Eloi jumped in the car to head back to Georgetown. It wasn't as unfashionable back then, like today, to drive after drinking.

Eloi was on the way home and just made the long turn near the entrance to the Brudenell Golf Course, when he noticed the RCMP had the lights flashing behind him. Eloi pulled over and the police officer approached the car, and shined the flashlight in.

"Oh, it's you John," the police officer said. "You are on the go late tonight."

In every Eloi story, he always referred to himself by his given name John. He never said Eloi. He told the men that he was closely connected with all the RCMP officers, though he never did mention how or why that connection would have been built.

Eloi went on to explain to the officer that he had been at a dance in Kilmuir and was now making the last part of the journey home to Georgetown.

"It's a dark old night, John," the police officer said. "Have you had anything to drink tonight John?"

Eloi looked the RCMP officer in the eye and said, "Officer I haven't had a drop of liquor all night."

The officer looked Eloi over and announced his presence was needed in the back of the squad car. Somewhat reluctantly, Eloi jumped in the back. The officer opened the glass window and handed Eloi a quart bottle of vodka, about three quarters full.

"Here John, take a snap out of that to help get you home!"

When he would tell us that, my father would burst into laughter and say, "Can you even imagine?" Then he'd laugh again.

Another time Dad told us they were sitting in the lunchroom at The Yard looking out over the frozen Georgetown Harbor. It was one of those winters that was very cold with little snow. One of the men mentioned that the ice was perfect for skating and that he might actually don the blades on the weekend.

Eloi told the lunch crew that he remembered back to when he was 16 or 17. It was a similar winter with a similar smooth sheet of ice in the harbor and he would often skate into Montague for groceries for his mother.

"I was a lovely skater," Eloi told them. "I remember Brigadeer Reid coming out from Charlottetown to watch me skate. 'John,' he said, 'you're the most beautiful skater I've ever laid my eyes on'. Brigadeer Reid coached Forbie Kennedy."

Eloi continued.

"I was some fast too. I was coming from Montague and I was carrying a small parcel for Mom under my coat. Evening was coming so I decided I would try to get home before it got too dark. After a few strides I was just flying. I felt the package shift so I unbuttoned my coat to adjust it. Didn't the wind pick up at that second and it caught my coat. Lord I was going so fast when I got to Georgetown I had to circle the red buoy three times to get stopped."

My father would laugh and say aloud, "John Doiron, quite a bucko he was."

The more outrageous the stories seemed, the more my father loved them. He told and re-told those stories for years after he retired from the Shipyard.

Looking back, I suppose my father always appreciated Eloi's ability to deliver a good story. I want to think my father understood the stories also represented Eloi's desire to fit in and be appreciated by his peers, but I will never know for sure.

One of the most powerful functions of a storyteller is the ability to transcend reality, to use words that free us from the mundane of ordinary life.

Few were as good at it as John Doiron.

It is hard for me to know where to start when it comes to explaining the incredible, unique person that was Mike Steele. Mike was my uncle by virtue of his marriage to my mother's youngest sister Betty Ann.

There was no one I have ever met before or since who had such a kind and giving heart. Even if it was to his own determent, he would go out of his way not to let you down. There was always a good turn in Mike Steele and he wore that like a badge of honor until the day he died.

And, he was a character unlike any other I have ever seen.

The Cowboy Mike Steele

Mike Steele was my father's best friend.

For as long as I can remember, he was called The Cowboy. Nobody really knew why since he didn't look like a cowboy. He never wore a cowboy hat or boots. And he never rode a horse. Regardless, the name just seemed to suit him to a tee.

Steele and my father went everywhere together. Ball games, hockey games, card plays, funerals, wakes and variety concerts. They would be gone just about every night. As we say in Georgetown, "they loved to run the roads."

They would bicker and argue like an old married couple. My father would criticize Steele for being late or having to leave a job early. He would torment Steele to the point where Mike would threaten my father's life a dozen times a day.

"You thin, grey son of a whore," he'd say to my father. "How would you like it if I drove this pulp hook into your forehead?"

Steele didn't mean it, of course. He was all bark and no bite. Dad knew this too and took no pass of it. It was just how they got along with each other - and they were inseparable.

Their friendship and partnership usually centered around some kind of project to make some extra money. That often meant going to the woods to cut pulp. They would find a piece of land to rent, and cut hardwood, softwood, pulpwood and logs.

If the property was close to the lumberyard in Georgetown, they would drag the wood by wagon or sleigh behind the tractor and weigh it in. Louis Gallant at the scale house would hate to see them coming as there would be less than half a cord in each load. It not only meant more bookwork for Louis, it meant more work as dad would ask him to get on the loader and unload it.

"Steady drops wear holes in rocks," Dad would tell us. It was kind of his way paraphrasing the Kentucky Fried Chicken commercial, *"another penny saved is another penny earned, that is something Colonel Sanders was mighty quick to learn."*

When you could get him on task, Steele was a tremendous worker. Dad knew this well. Dad had become quite crippled up with arthritis in later years and without Steele, there would have been no logs to sell. Steele's participation was critical to the operation and he was generally good to show up for work every day. Except Thursdays.

Thursday was, and remains, provincial court day at the Kings County Courthouse in Georgetown. Steele never missed court. In fact, he had become such a fixture in the courthouse that when Justice Bertrand Plamandon would enter through the front door, with two fingers balancing the hanger holding his robes on his shoulder, he would say, "Good Morning Mr. Steele." Steele would wave or acknowledge the judge before taking his seat on a front bench.

Steele had tremendous respect for Lady Justice and the procedures of the court. He would sit quietly, legs crossed with both hands resting on his lap, just taking everything in. Sometimes he would wear his Sunday best, other times he would stroll in with work pants and a ball hat. However, he was polite enough to remove his hat before entering the courtroom. Anyone that knew Mike Steele knew he was always kind and polite.

One day there was trial scheduled. It had involved a young lad from the area who had been nabbed for "bad breath," the local slang term for an impaired driving charge. The details were sketchy but the arresting officer was only a few months on the job with the RCMP. The accused felt the arrest hadn't been cleanly handled and felt there was a chance he could get off on a technicality, so he had pleaded not guilty.

A lawyer from Montague had been retained by the accused - a short and self-important man known to be dogged with witnesses. When this lawyer would ask a question, he would purse his lips and shake his head feverishly. It was part condescending, part confidence, and all for effect. The Crown Attorney was familiar with his foe and painstaking effort had gone into preparing the young RCMP officer for his time on the witness stand.

The Crown Attorney felt confident about the case - that it would be a slam-dunk, providing the young officer could hold up under cross-examination and so he was coached to carefully listen to and consider each question from the defense lawyer. The young man was reminded, time and again, to think clearly before answering. After considerable preparation, it was time for the witness to take the stand.

The Montague lawyer asked a number of simple yes and no questions to loosen up the witness. Then the questions became longer and more probing. At one point, the lawyer asked, "On the date in question, you are alleged to have witnessed the accused operating a motor vehicle while under impairment. Would the accused be in the court room today, and if so, could the witness please point to him?"

Now, the young RCMP officer felt this was a very innocuous question, but he remembered his pre-trial coaching. The question seemed almost too simple, so he didn't answer. He waited.

After a long silence, the defense lawyer asked the same question. He asked the witness to point to the accused. Again the young officer was spellbound. After what seemed like an eternity, the young officer lifted his right hand, extended his index finger and started to move his arm back and forth in front of the crowd that had gathered in the courtroom. Obviously confused and now downright terrified, he began to move his arm faster and faster, side to side, before slowing it down and stopping.

The officer was pointing directly at Mike Steele. Steele was gobsmacked but undeterred. He looked right at the officer and spoke.

"Oh no dear. It's not me dear. That's him right over there dear!"

The courtroom erupted. I think even Judge Plamandon smiled.

It was classic Mike Steele.

Many years later, on the night my father died, nobody cried harder than Mike Steele. Every time I saw him after my father had passed, Steele would share a little story or memory. He would ask me to tell him something that would make him laugh and I would. He would slap his leg, open his mouth, throw his head back and laugh loudly. Eventually the laughter would subside and big tears would start to roll down his cheeks.

He would always say of my father, "My Jesus, he's an awful miss."

Steele lived most of his life in poor health, battling skin cancer for more than 30 years. His face was scarred and parts of his lips and mouth had been removed, but he never let it bother him - or change him.

As he always did, Steele continued to run the roads. One evening he was attending a ceilidh dance in Charlottetown. After dancing for hours he went outside for a cigarette and suffered a massive heart attack. He was dead before he hit the ground.

Steele too, is an awful miss.

I loved when my father would tell us stories about a man named Mackey.

Mackey was married to Sophia. When my father said her name in his best Mackey voice, he would draw it out "SoFFIIIIIaaa." They had a big family, they were very well thought of by neighbours and so many of their legendary stories have been told and re-told for decades.

Mackey and Sophia

One time Mackey had a severe case of the piles (hemorrhoids) and was having trouble just staying seated. He asked his wife Sophia to get the salve from the medicine cabinet in the bathroom. Sophia returned and handed a tube to Mackey, which he proceeded to use to soothe the pain in his behind.

Mackey put one dab on his swollen piles and he almost hit the roof. He began to roar and shout and scream, took off on the dead run and jumped out through the picture window in the living room. Mackey put his bare arse in the snow bank.

When she looked at the package on the table, Sophia realized she had given Mackey some Minard's Linament.

Half naked in the snow, Mackey roared out, "SooFFFIIIIaaa!"

Another time, my father told me about the family sitting around the supper table. Sophia had just made fresh bread. Paul, one of the sons, was very much enjoying the bread. As fast as his mother was cutting it, Paul would butter it, eat it and announce, "Cut me another slice momma."

This continued for several minutes. Paul would eat a slice, look at Sophia and repeat, "Cut me another slice, Momma."

Having witnessed this for long enough, Mackey interrupted and said, "Cut his f@#%in' throat, Momma!"

My favorite Mackey story of all was one I heard only recently. It involved a couple of his sons, Stevie and Terry. The boys were jigging around the kitchen and thought they saw a shadow in the gap between the floor and chimney. They figured it was a mouse or rat. A few minutes later, they noticed it again. The shadow seemed big enough to be a rat, so Terry told Stevie to go get the hammer. They planned to sit silently by the gap until they saw the shadow and Stevie would clunk it with the hammer.

After waiting a few minutes, the shadow re-appeared and Stevie swung the hammer for all he was worth. There was a big thud in the basement. The boys ran down to see what had happened and they saw Mackey laying on the clay floor. He had been down cleaning the stove and when he got up to take the tray of ashes outside, Stevie pounded him in the head with the hammer. Mackey was knocked unconscious.

Stevie was in shock. After a few minutes, he asked Terry what he should do. Terry offered the best advice he could and he saw no need to sugar coat it.

"If I were you, I'd run!"

Howard MacLean was another well-known and well-respected resident of Georgetown. He was known far-and-wide by his nickname, Binx. His brother Walter was "Blinky." Georgetown is famous for great nicknames, as the MacLean brothers could attest.

The Guy Called Binx MacLean

Binx MacLean served around the municipal government for years and was also one to be part of community groups like the Lions Club. He was a community-first type of person and by all accounts one of the leaders of the town for many years.

Binx was also very handy, with years of experience as an electrician. Like many of his age, he had an inquiring mind when it came to creating things and could, as they often said, turn his hand to just about anything.

The MacLean home would have been one of the first you would see as you entered the town of Georgetown, prior to the construction of "the new houses", a low rental housing project built in the late 1970s - now more than 40 years old, but still referred to by locals as "the new houses."

Though certainly not one to be persnickety by nature, Binx could have a short fuse and never liked to be bothered when he was tinkering with a gadget or trying to concentrate on the job at hand.

One evening in the late fall, Binx found himself up on the roof of his two-story home, fiddling with the television antenna. It would be a delicate job at the best of times, being up on the steep roof. The fall wind combined with the evening darkness only added to the challenge. Needless to say, it wouldn't have been a good time to bother Binx with anything but a full-blown town emergency.

This never deterred Merrick Easton, another of the many characters that called Georgetown home. Merrick was a practical joker of high regard and always found pleasure in playing a gag on friends. Merrick had driven by the MacLean house and noticed Binx on the roof. He figured Binx would not want to be bothered, which is exactly why Merrick decided to do just that.

The Eastons were well-known traders and barterers. They would often land home with truckloads of used clothing from the Boston states and sell them piece by piece to the townsfolk. For years, it was the only clothing worn by anyone from Georgetown. Merrick went home and worked up a costume so that he looked like an important business man from out of town. He went back to see Binx.

Merrick pulled in the driveway and in an altered voice began to shout, "Ooohh Mr. MacLean. I would like to speak to Mr. MacLean."

Binx could hear something and immediately shouted back.

"I'm terrible busy here, what do you want?"

Merrick announced that he was there to inquire about the price of the house.

Binx was confused.

"The price of what house? This house isn't for sale, now fly the Jesus out of here."

Merrick was giggling to himself. He was enjoying himself far too much to stop.

"Mr. MacLean, I've been informed this house is for sale and I represent a client who would love to buy it."

Binx was fuming, his voice getting higher and more agitated.

"I already told you, fly the Jesus out of here. This house is not for sale."

Merrick was almost fainting, doing all he could to hold in the laugh.

"Mr. MacLean, I've been told this house is for sale and my client is prepared to pay you $125,000 for it."

Binx roared from the roof.

"I will be right down!"

My brother Mark and I pretty much grew up at the MacConnell home on the corner of Victoria and Grafton Streets in Georgetown. The home was the scene of many crimes, endless laughs, bloody fights, and every other bit of treachery that bold kids could manage to think up. It was the centre of our world. It was the happiest place I have ever known.

The matriarch of the MacConnell house was Flossie. She was our mother's sister. We never had to ask to stay over. The little bungalow was already home to 13 kids and I guess Flossie figured two or three more crammed in would not make much difference. We just slept where we dropped.

Whenever there was a threat of a snowstorm, we would beg our father to drive us to Flossie's so we could get storm stayed (a well known Atlantic Canadian term for being snowed in). One time the power went out for a week. The provisions in the house were pretty much picked over, and I do not think we ate for two days at the end, but they were the best days of our lives!

The Long, Ol' Drive with Charlie MacConnell

Our Aunt Flossie was married to Charlie MacConnell. He was mostly very quiet and would have been largely a stoic symbol of our youth.

If we needed a drive somewhere, Charlie would take us. But, other than that, he'd watch a lot of TV or read westerns. He pretty much kept to himself, and since he was a big man with a loud roar that would almost make you poop in your pants, we were glad that he did.

I was in my 20s before I found out Charlie was a veteran of World War II. Charlie served as part of the Royal Hamilton Light Infantry. He was a foot soldier. He never talked about his time in the war. He never went to the Remembrance Day celebrations. I suppose, like many soldiers it was a time he would have rather not remembered.

His son, my cousin Brad, grew up, followed his father's footsteps and enlisted in the military. He became a military policeman. Brad began to appreciate his father's military service and spent a great deal of time researching the military records. He had planned to try, as best he could, to re-trace his father's journey through Europe in the early 1940s.

It took Brad a few years but he was able to comb through the miles of paperwork. One Christmas he presented Charlie with a plane ticket. Brad was going to take him back to Europe and they were going to re-trace the journey together. Brad knew his Dad would need re-enforcements, so it was determined Brad's father-in-law Stewart MacRae and Charlie's brother Jimmy would be part of the trip.

They flew to Europe, rented a car and had a truly marvellous adventure. One day, towards the end of the trip, they had left Germany and were driving to the hotel they had booked in France. It had been a long day on the road and the conversation had pretty much dried up.

Brad was at the wheel. As he drove down the dark road, he looked in the back and saw Jimmy's head was leaning on the window, his *MacLean's Ready Mix* cap was tipped forward and he was fast asleep. Brad looked over to the other side of the car and noticed that Stewart's head was bobbing up and down. His father-in-law was about to start snoring.

Brad then looked over at his father. Charlie had reclined the front seat a bit and was having difficulty keeping his eyes open. The significance of the moment had overtaken Brad. His father was in his advanced years and Brad felt very grateful to have been able to put together such a poignant journey. His father was not the type of person to say so, but Brad knew Charlie felt the same way.

Just then, Brad took his right hand off the wheel and lightly patted his father's leg.

"She's a long old drive, eh Pop," Brad said.

Charlie opened up one eye and softly said.

"Try walkin' 'er!"

Part 6: Personal Favorites and other Classics

While Georgetown has many great and unique characters, so too do many of the other communities in the eastern of PEI and the entire Island in general.

One of the great characters is Bobby Fraser just outside of St. Peters. Bobby has been immortalized in song by my good friend Eddy Quinn, whose song, "Bobby and the Bear" chronicles the legendary night when Bobby entered the ring at Iceland Arena in Montague to wrestle a brown bear. It was part of the Atlantic Grand Prix Wrestling shenanigans in the early 1980s.

It's funny how legends grow. I was a regular fan at the wrestling matches. On a good night there would be 300-400 people in the stands. Often times less. But if you were to go around Kings County, every single person you would ask would tell you that they were at the rink the night Bobby wrestled the bear. Full to the rafters, the rink would hold about 1,200. That night, as the legend has grown, there must have been 22,000.

There are many great "Bobby" stories. This one, wrestling bears aside, is as good as any I've heard. It not only defines what a great character Bobby is, it underlines his blue-collar work ethic and validates his rural authenticity of having "no airs about him."

Bobby and the Million

Not long after the Atlantic Lotto started to become fashionable there was a big draw for a one million dollars. It was unheard of at the time but as you might expect, the Island was in a tizzy. The draw was simply known as, "the million." In my memory, this predates the Lotto 6/49, but it had a similar impact on the news cycle and community gossip that you would see when the Powerball Lottery hits $700 million in the US.

A common conversation at the grocery store as you waited in line to buy a ticket would be the inevitable, "What would you do if you won the million?" The corner store in St. Peters was no exception the day Bobby came in to try his luck.

Bobby laid down his money and after he was presented his tickets, the store clerk asked what he might do if he won the million. Bobby never hesitated.

"I'd go straight to Charlottetown and buy two brand new Husqvarna chain saws. I'd be all done going to the woods with a poor saw!"

Since I began telling stories on stage, I seem to run into people more often who are quick to share a story of their own. Sometimes the stories can be downright torturous, but I always laugh or smile and thank the person for sharing. Sometimes, you get a gem. Over the years, I have observed that good storytellers know a good story when they hear one, as was the case one day in Charlottetown when I gathered for lunch with my brother Mark, my friend and storytelling colleague Gary Evans, and my cousin Brad MacConnell.

After sharing a few laughs and idle chit-chat, Brad announced he had a good story for us. He proceeded to tell this one about his father-in-law Stewart MacRae from Point Prim. As Brad was telling this story, Gary and I made eye contact. Both of us knew it was a dandy! Both of us were already working the story through our minds to "make it our own," as storytellers often do. I am glad I beat Gary to the punch on this one!

A Trip to the Doctor with Stewart MacRae

Stewart MacRae is a quiet family man from Point Prim. He is rural and authentic. He talks with a great Island twang and enjoys a good laugh. Stewart was born and raised in Point Prim. He and his wife Barb also raised their own family there. After a long career with the Island Telephone Company, Stewart retired and opened a tourism cottage business on the family property.

More than 20 years ago, my cousin Brad married Stewart's oldest daughter Kerri-Lee. Everyone calls her Kiki. Brad was welcomed with open arms into the MacRae family and over the years, as sons-in-law often do, he wound up helping out the family when they needed it.

Such was the case one day when Kiki's mother, Barb, called and asked if Brad could take Stewart into Charlottetown for a doctor's appointment. Brad, never wanting to say no to his mother-in-law, agreed and set off to Point Prim for the pickup. Brad was aware Stewart was having some health problems, but wasn't totally up to speed as to the severity of the issues. He also didn't want to question Stewart on the drive in to the city, so he just went about regular small talk, content on making sure all of the needs of the patient were adhered to.

Stewart is a prototypical rural Islander. He didn't get to town all that often and would always look forward to the trip. He loved to go to town and walk around, whistling a bit as he walked, taking in the sights, looking over the strangers and hoping to God to run into someone he knew for a short chat.

Stewart loved to chat. In fact, he wouldn't necessarily need to know your name to strike up a conversation. If he were to see a friendly face and a willing participant, Stewart would chat about anything and everything.

Stewart's appointment was at the Polyclinic Professional Centre in Charlottetown, an office building where a number of doctors see patients daily. Brad parked the car and walked beside him as they climbed the steps to the building. Stewart nodded at a passerby and said hello to a man leaving - someone he didn't really know.

Once inside, Stewart announced to Brad that he had to use the washroom. Brad was uncertain of his father-in-law's condition, so he started to follow him into the washroom. Stewart stopped

Brad and indicated, by holding up two fingers, that job he was about to do would be best done in private. Brad gladly backed off.

Stewart walked into one of the stalls. As he sat down he heard a voice in the next stall say, "And how are you today?"

Stewart looked around, shrugged his shoulders and not wanting to be impolite, responded.

"Well, I guess I'm not too bad, all things considered."

The voice in the next stall continued, in a more hushed tone.

"Well, that's great to hear. How long are you going to be in town?"

Stewart thought for a second, wanting to provide accurate information.

"I have to go see the doctor here, hope to God it doesn't take more than 20 minutes."

Says the voice, getting even lower, to the point where it's almost a whisper.

"How long will it be before you head for home?"

Again, Stewart paused, going over in his mind the couple of little errands he had to complete after seeing the doctor.

"I figure we will finish here, stop at the grocery store for a couple of things and then another 25 minutes or so for the drive home. All things considered, I'm pretty sure we should be home just before supper. The wife has a ham on."

Silence fell over the other stall. After a few seconds, Stewart bent his ear gently toward the stall, hoping to confirm his new friend hadn't passed out - or worse. After a few moments, the voice started again, this time quite a bit louder.

"Listen, I'm going to have to let you go here. Some arsehole is in the other stall and he thinks I am talking to him!"

I had the great pleasure to appear on stage with legendary Hockey Night in Canada host Ron MacLean. MacLean was headlining a fundraising event for the University of Prince Edward Island Panthers Men's hockey program. I was asked to serve as the opening act, a rather difficult task considering guests paid their money to see the likeable MacLean.

I thought it was important to try to get a few laughs and keep the room in a jubilant mood. I also wanted to ensure our special guest was entertained. I knew MacLean loved PEI and had become close friends with

members of the famed Kennedy family – the Island's first family of hockey.

After wracking my brain for what seemed like hours, I remembered this

hilarious story my friend Kenny MacDougall told me about Forbie

Kennedy, the first PEI hockey player to make a career in the NHL.

Just Being Forbie Kennedy

Forbes Kennedy made a living being an aggressive, heart
and soul hockey player for a number of NHL teams. He made the
National Hockey League when there were only six teams, which
gives you an indication of just how good a player he was. He was,
and is, a PEI hockey legend. Far and wide, he's known as Forbie.

Forbie still owns the NHL record for having the most
penalty minutes in a playoff game. His team, the Leafs, were being
pummeled by the Boston Bruins. Leafs coach Punch Imlach tapped
Forbie on the leg and said, "Go start something." What ensued is a
now legendary battle royal. Forbie fought four or five times,
knocked down a linesman in a brawl that last more than a half
hour. When he returned to the Leafs room bloodied and battered,

Forbie was approached by Imlach who said, "I told you to start *something*, not World War III!"

There was also the time Forbie was recruited to play with the Halifax Jr. Canadiens. Forbie had been a dominant player on the Island, playing against men twice his age. He was leaving the Island for the first time. He took the train to Halifax where he was to be met by a member of the Canadiens staff. Forbie got off the train and was looking around the Halifax station when a man with a suit approached him.

The man, inquiring as to which hotel the youngster was heading, asked "Lord Nelson?"

Forbie innocently replied, "No sir. Forbes Taylor Kennedy."

Forbie has always been sincere, upfront and honest. There are no airs about him and he has always been true to his roots. What you see is what you get and he makes no apologies for it. Forbie not only wears his heart on his sleeve, he puts all of it into everything he does. The only way he knows how to do things is his way.

After his playing career, Forbie became a successful coach. His teams played as he did - tough, hard and determined. He coached many PEI and Atlantic championship teams. Though he wouldn't hesitate to address a player with passionate, colorful language, Forbie was universally loved by all who played for him.

As he got older, though the game of hockey changed, Forbie remained the same. Toward the end of his coaching career, he was leading a young tier II junior team in Summerside. As Forbie walked into the arena for practice, the team's general manager Gabe Keough pulled the coach aside.

Keough explained that he had been hearing some complaints from some of the parents of the younger players, that Forbie was being pretty tough on some of the kids and was using language that would make a drunken sailor blush. Keough tried to tip-toe around the issue by suggesting the game of hockey was changing drastically, and that perhaps it was time for the old coach to adapt along with it.

Forbie chucked his cigar into his mouth and told his GM that he understood.

"Get all the boys in the dressing room Gabe and we will address this right now," Forbie said.

Keough did as he was asked and after a quick roll call, he closed the door and leaned his back against it. Forbie moved to the centre of the room and politely asked Keough to leave.

"Thanks Gabe, but this is something that has to be handled between the players and the coach."

Dutifully, Keough stepped outside. Forbie looked around the room and a mean scowl came over his face.

"OK boys," he said angrily. "Seems we got a f@#&in' rat in here!"

The game of hockey may have changed, but Forbie Kennedy will always be the same.

Growing up, it seemed almost every rural family had a story, or knew a story, that involved a rushed wedding date or the birth of a child that occurred not long after nuptials had been exchanged.

It was conventional for the times to "glaze over" these finer points. Most families would never have any discussions about the "why" or "how" of family making. Sometimes a child would become brave or bold enough to ask, only to be shot down by parents. There were some parents who became quite skillful at answering the dicey questions, as evidenced in this story.

The Birds and the Bees

One day, a young fellow in the Georgetown area was reviewing the ages and birthdays of his six siblings. He had never been curious before about such things, but growing into a young man, he was beginning to think at a different level.

He had long known his parents had been married in November of 1957. He had also long known his oldest brother was born in 1958. As be began to do the math in his head, he realized his brother had been born only six months after his parents wed.

Although the young man thought he had it figured out, he was still naïve enough to be doubtful. He had gained just enough life confidence that he felt comfortable trying to broach the topic.

One evening after supper, he approached his mother in the kitchen and stated, "You guys were married in November, but John was born six months later. How do you explain that?"

The mother wiped her hands on the beige apron she was wearing, and continued to go about her business as if unfazed. She grabbed the remaining dishes off the table and answered her son's question as she moved to the sink.

"Well now dear," she said. "The first baby can come anytime. All the rest after that take nine months."

My friend Leo Walsh from Watervale, PEI is a political animal. Like the generations of Walshes before him, he is proudly Irish, staunchly Catholic and faithfully Tory.

Leo enjoys a good laugh as much as anyone I have known. One day over lunch, he told me this little anecdote about the first time Leo and his wife Joan, freshly married, talked about politics.

Exercising Your Watervale Franchise

There was a provincial election on, and late in the afternoon of voting day Leo and Joan drove to the poll to exercise their franchise. Before they got out of the car, Leo grabbed softly onto her wrist and in a round-about way tried to ask Joan what she was going to do inside the polling station.

Joan wasn't quick to answer, and Leo was cute enough to know he wasn't going to get very far being brazen. He thought for a moment and offered the same advice to Joan that his own father Chester offered many years earlier to his new bride.

"Sometimes we vote for the man, and sometimes we vote for the party. But the Walshes always find a way to vote Tory!"

Most of the people I grew up with in Georgetown lived very modestly. Some had even less. When you consider the excesses most middle-income families enjoy now, some of the older, "we were so poor" stories make you wonder how some people even survived.

In the late 1970s, a large number of people from Newfoundland and Labrador came to Georgetown to work at the fish plant. Their new location was very similar to home in attitude and sense of community. They also shared the sharp wit and keen sense of humor so rampant in Georgetown.

The town fit some so well. Many stayed, married locally and raised their families here. As a high school student, my brother Lloyd and his friends worked at the fish plant and become lifelong friends of many. He recalls and tells hilarious stories about those times, including this one about his friend Wilfred.

Stretching the Gifted Turkey

Wilfred came from a big family in Burgeo, Newfoundland. Like most families in the area, the family worked in the fishery and did its best to make ends meet. And, like many in the community, Wilfred's family didn't have much more than the bare necessities.

Often at break time at the plant, many of the young men would gather and talk about all things rural, quite often how families in the 1950s and 60s, be it PEI or Newfoundland, had to be resourceful and learn how to stretch provisions on a daily basis. Wilfred claimed his mother was as resourceful as they come.

One time near Christmas, a neighbor stopped by their house and in keeping with the kindness of the season, dropped off a large turkey. It weighed about 25 or 30 pounds. Wilfred's mother was grateful for the bounty and immediately prepared it for the oven. It had been a difficult stretch for the family and his mom knew she had to make the best of it.

Wilfred flipped over a five-gallon bucket, sat on it and explained to the lunchroom crowd:

"On Sunday we had a full-blown turkey dinner with potatoes and vegetables. On Monday, Mom used some of the leftovers to make a hash. On Tuesday, we had open-faced hot turkey sandwiches. On Wednesday, she whipped together some turkey salad sandwiches. On Thursday, Mom boiled the bones and we had turkey soup. And on Friday, whatever was left of it, she used to make fish cakes!"

My friend John Eden and I had lunch one day in Charlottetown. John has always gotten a great charge out of my rural Island accent and my stories, dating back to the mid-1990s when he hired me to work at CFCY radio station.

I told him a few stories and then he swung one back at me. Although it is a story from Gaspe, Quebec, it struck a chord with me because it has similarities to stories from rural communities of my youth. It is also symbolic of the wholesome, innocent nature of rural, east coast Canadians.

In small communities, the few who manage to get a college education tend to be held in high regard. It would be common for them to be asked to assist others with topics outside of their field of study, but since they "went to school," they were deemed to be supremely qualified.

The Eaton's catalogue

Mary had recently returned home for Christmas break from Dalhousie University, where she was studying towards a Bachelor of Arts degree. Mary was a quiet young woman who rarely circulated. Therefore, she was surprised to open her parents' front door one day to find an elderly lady who was kindly requesting an audience with her.

Mary recognized the lady as Mrs. Roberts, owner of a farm about three miles to the south. In her entire life, Mary had never had any significant interaction with Mrs. Roberts outside of a casual hello at the corner store. Being neighborly, Mary invited her visitor inside.

Mrs. Roberts went straight to the kitchen table and set her carrying bag down. She opened it, and pulled out the Eaton's catalogue. She set the catalogue down, folded her hands on top of it, and informed Mary that her assistance was required to order a Christmas present for Mr. Roberts.

Mrs. Roberts told Mary that she found the Eaton's ordering process to be confusing, and felt more comfortable getting help from "someone with a Dalhousie education." Mary did not understand why such a simple task could lead to confusion, but not wanting to be unfriendly, she agreed to assist with ordering the gift.

Mary thumbed through the catalogue until she found the men's wear pages. Mrs. Roberts smiled. Mary nodded and reached into the back page, pulled out the perforated order sheet, and put it flat on the table. Mary then fetched a pen, and asked Mrs. Roberts to explain the exact details of the order.

It was not quite the answer Mary had been expecting.

"I'm looking for a nice, white shirt for a lovely man named Harold!"

Endorsements

Ron MacLean, host, Hockey Night in Canada

"To know France, you must know something about wine. With Canada, It's hockey. And PEI? You have to know about the Kennedy family - Brad Richards made sure I understood this.... And you must know about Dennis King!"

Paul MacNeill, Publisher, Island Press Ltd.

"Dennis King is an expert storyteller who unabashedly celebrates the personalities and quirks of the people who surrounded him as a child. Growing up in Georgetown, PEI it would be easy to feel the grass is always greener on the other side. While the economy often sagged and industries came and went, the people of this hardscrabble town never lost their pride in place. If you were born there, you will always call it home. King's stories, some perhaps embellished for effect, revel in the memories made during a simpler time, before the Internet and video games. His collection of stories is belly laugh funny. Most importantly it is a love story to a town that remains unique to this day."

Kerri Wynne MacLeod, host, Ocean 100 morning show

"Our 30 year friendship has been nurtured through hilarity, quenched with clever wit, and fed a regular diet of realistic (and often twisted!) humor that only comes from being able to laugh at ourselves - as Islanders and the indigenous peoples of the great Kings County! If laughter really is the best medicine, then Dennis is one of my favorite drug dealers. God love 'em! Holy Dinah! Man, dear!"

Hon. Robert Ghiz, 31st Premier of Prince Edward Island

"Dennis King is what I would call an Island character. He grew up in Kings County, has worked in Charlottetown, married a girl from Prince County and now lives in rural Queens County. You could say that he is a bit like our Island newspaper The Guardian - he covers the Island like the dew.

With this understanding of the Island it is no surprise that Dennis has become one of the eminent storytellers in Prince Edward Island. Also, he's supposedly a fine athlete and one of the biggest supporters of local sports on the Island. And to top it all off he's an aberration in Island politics- he's was born a Liberal and turned Conservative!

With his great sense of humor and ability to deliver one liners this should be quite the book!"

Doug MacLean, former newspaper columnist

"I was thrilled to hear Dennis was putting together a book of stories. I have known the King family for a long time and Dennis comes by his talents honestly. His uncle Donald was a gifted storyteller, writer and poet. Only the late, great Urban Carmichael, for possessing a quick wit and an ability to tell a tale, rivals Dennis' father, the legendary Lionel. This book is a must-read for me."

Allan Andrews, President, Andrews Hockey Growth Programs

"Having grown up on a small, mixed farm with seven siblings myself, the stories that Dennis King relates in his book bring me back to a time when life was simple, friends were treasured and evenings were story time. Denny is a true grassroots historian – entertaining us with tales that can make us laugh and cry. I am privileged to be able to call him friend."

Myron Yates, former teacher and principal

"Through the influences of a loving family and friends, Dennis King recounts personal memories of coming of age as a young boy growing up in a small town. Dennis recalls observations of a lifetime weaving poignant and humorous anecdotes into an entertaining collection of stories, which celebrate the people who have influenced him as a writer. Though generated in the warm interactions among people living in a

185

tight-knit rural community, the stories embody a larger meaning in the broader context of our lives. Through a series of mishaps, misunderstanding and good intentions gone astray, the characters reveal a side of human life, which creates joyful recollections and significant life lessons long after the initial event.

Stories give meaning to our lives and Dennis' gift to the reader is that of appreciating those who cause us to reflect on context behind the actions we observe."

Myrtle Jenkins-Smith, life-long family friend

"When I heard that Dennis was publishing a book about classic Georgetown characters and stories, I started chuckling to myself thinking that Dennis himself is a classic story-telling character. How fitting for him to be writing a book on that very subject.

The King and Jenkins families have been connected for generations. When Dennis was younger, he was at our house for so many meals and sleepovers he blended right in with the dozen Jenkins kids very well. He loved to listen to my Dad Hibbie tell stories and jokes.

Lionel King, Dennis' father, was another great, Georgetown character. I spent many evenings listening to Lionel hold court telling classic stories that kept us all in stitches, so, the apple never fell far from the tree.

I am so pleased that Dennis is keeping the story-telling tradition alive. This gifted story-telling character is also preserving the history of the place where we grew up and are proud to call home - Georgetown."

Alan Buchanan, master storyteller

"The key to great story telling is a good ear. All the best storytellers have it: an ability to hear a story where others only hear a narrative. Dennis King has it in spades, and that is what comes through loud and clear in this very personal collection of stories from his hometown of Georgetown. Dennis hears "the story" in every neighbor's voice and in every quirky, funny, and touchingly poignant incident, that illustrates the everyday life of a small town. Their stories are all here...told with a love and respect and an understanding that can only come from having been an intimate part of it all. Dennis' pride of place comes shining through, and in almost every story, the hero is Georgetown. If you love the stories of Stephen Leacock, Garrison Keillor, or Stuart McLean, you'll love the stories of Dennis King."

Matt Rainnie, host, Island Morning Show, CBC Radio

"A good story is like a flavorful, nourishing meal and it all begins with a recipe. The storyteller must be a keen observer and attentive listener. They have to care deeply about their subject. They have to have a way with words, a gift for gab. Dennis King is a natural. His love of PEI and its people radiates from his stories, as does his sense of humor. Like all the best chefs, Dennis adds a little magic to the dish that's hard to duplicate but a pleasure to taste."

Acknowledgements

I wish to thank the many people who encouraged me to share my stories, and who supported me through the exhaustive process of publishing a book. I could have not have completed this without their help:

My wife, and editor, Jana Hemphill for her invaluable expertise with layout, design and critique. It wasn't an easy task. Writers are hyper-sensitive and protective of their choice of words. Husbands that are writers even more so. I wanted the unique voice and phrasing of my hometown to shine through in this book. Jana helped to make that happen.

My children Jake, Camdyn and Callum who practised great patience to allow their Dad the extra time to focus on writing. They are the joys of my life.

Dennis Curley, fellow author, long-time family friend and my namesake, for reading through the original draft of my work and suggesting edits and improvements. The miles separate us, but stories continue to connect us.

Myron Yates, my Grade 8 teacher and the first person who recognized my writing ability. He told me to put my pencil on the paper and let the magic happen. I have been following that advice ever since. His endorsement for my book touched me so much that I included in on the back cover.

My Four Tellers family - Gary Evans, Alan Buchanan, David Weale and behind the scenes fifth teller Colin Buchanan – to have been given a seat at the storytelling table with you has been rewarding and one pile of fun. It has been a privilege.

Photographer and fellow Georgetonian Cheryl Perry for working her magic and making me look presentable for this book; as well as the talented and patient Aura Lee Shepard, who was able to take a muddy concept from my mind and turn it into a wonderful book cover.

To Faye Rilley, Georgetown's official photographer and modern-day historian, for providing great pictures of great characters. Thanks for doing what you do!

My friend Melissa Batchilder, who has a heart as big as a horse bucket, for her constant belief in our hometown, and me. She understands the wonderment of a story and its powers to unite.

To all of those who wrote endorsements, supported and encouraged me to get this book to print, I thank you for your advice and friendship.

To my good friend and fellow author Eddy Quinn for giving me an invaluable list of dos and don'ts that helped me immensely in the publishing process.

To my extended King family, namely Heather (King) Pankratz and Chris (King) Flynn for working with me to share some of the stories and poems of Uncle Donald and Uncle Jack. I hope somewhere the King brothers are smiling and still trying to outdo one another with stories.

To Brady and Joe MacConnell, and Derek Johnson, my best friends for life and the source of so much laughter (and mental anguish!) for the past 40 years. I hope and pray for 40 more!

To the descendants of Boughton Island, I hope this book, in some small way, is able to capture the magic and heart of that most special place.

My mother Cattie, the rock of our family and one of the key historical sources for many of these stories. The walk down memory lane has been entertaining and emotional – but I will forever treasure the journey. Love ya Cat!

To my brothers Benji, Lloyd, Mark and sisters Peggy, Pammy, Toby and Susie – my biggest fans and the people who are forever laughing with me. I thank them for being good sports and for not putting up too much fuss as intimate details of their lives are shared with strangers. Together we make great stories.

And, to all of the people who have, or still call Georgetown home. We may not realize it often enough, but we live in the greatest little town in the world. It is a town of characters and a town with character. I hope this book provides an adequate depiction of the love and appreciation I have for "the big G."

To book Denny for an event:

mdennyking7@gmail.com

(902) 314-6229

Or visit:

www.dennyking.ca